Decoding the Mystery of Life After Life

Passage to the Beyond, Near-Death Experiences, and Unveiling of the Afterlife's Mysteries

Joyce T.

Copyright

errors, omissions, or misinterpretations within the subject matter presented herein.

Contents

Introduction

This I choose to do. If there is a price, this I choose to pay. If it is my death, then I choose to die. Where this takes me, there I choose to go. I choose. This I choose to do. –Terry Pratchett

Y ou've picked up this book thanks to your strong sense of appreciation for the air you breathe and the roads you travel, haven't you?

Nothing changes our view on living as much as a near-death experience (NDE) does. Of the countless types of life events, death is one that we know all manners of living creatures surely face. But miraculous survivors momentarily gain a world's worth of emotions within a fraction of a second and are truly humbled.

This is what I bring you, reader! *Decoding the Mystery of Life After Life* is a book based on my experiences and lessons. Contemplating death and the beyond is a task we—from philosophers to children and experts to novices—engage in.

The final question differs from person to person, but in the end, we always wonder about the philosophy and reality of the Grim Reaper and what great adventure they may lead us on.

Famed comedian and actor Tracy Morgan survived a car crash in 2014, was in a coma for a couple of weeks, and woke up to the news that his good friend, James McNair, had passed away in that wreck. Months of treatment, therapy, and support gave Morgan the strength to explain what it means to have survived and live again (Diaz, 2015):

> Well, you're never going to be normal after you go through something like that. You don't die for a few weeks and then come back to normal, trust me. Something's going to be missing, something's going to be gained—you just got to live your life after that. (para. 5)

Perhaps normal is overrated. But I'll tell you right now, *you* get to decide what's normal. You get to make new choices and heart-pumping decisions. Surviving such an event is an unfathomable thing for so many, and yet, the world keeps turning and you move with it. There's no saying how things will turn out, but when you wake back up to life, it's a journey to find peace and keep going.

The Questions and Answers

Having an NDE and understanding the fluidity of the afterlife (defined differently by thousands of faiths) are some of life's most precious moments. With this book, you can recognize, understand, and accept these trials as lessons.

These hair-raising events involve potential bouts of relief. The book will explore this in detail, delving into the methods of personal growth and transformation. We are forever altered by harrowing experiences, but with careful practice and consideration, we can direct our own path to recovery. How do we achieve this?

First. give yourself time and space to process the event. An NDE is nothing to shrug off. When possible, reflect on the emotions that arise from such a moment. It's always important to make the effort to engage in deep contemplation since this allows you to gradually regain clarity.

Find opportunities to work on short-term motivations and security. An NDE, for example, brings drastic shifts to your understanding and priorities in life. Many people go on to lead more fulfilling lives when they've escaped narrow circumstances. It's not an instinctual change but the result of strong self-reflection and hard-won wisdom.

Best of all, healing involves seeking help from trusted people. Whether they're close folks from your inner circle or professional counselors and online communities, humanity is rife with people ready to help each other out.

By connecting with support groups and the like, you are introduced to a host of new information and perspectives from shockingly similar experiences others have had. They strengthen the bonds of community and offer validation. The right people recognize that your pain is real and must be felt. That is how you know you're healing.

The Journey

Alongside the struggles and pain of recovery, this book covers the possibilities of past-life regression, out-of-body experiences, and our journey beyond the veil. It's fascinating to uncover and explore stories of the afterlife. Many are about catharsis, happy endings, and second chances. When our ancestors wrote about what lay beyond death, they injected morality, love, and hope into their tales.

We will never find straightforward solutions. But that's the point of life's adventure!

The conjectures that run in myths, generational stories, long-lasting cultures, and religious texts define the afterlife in intricate and unique ways. But we can never be sure of the theories closest to the real deal. In my opinion, it's not the answer but the discussions that are worthy of exploration.

We see this in funeral rituals, memorial services, and mourning traditions as well. These practices vary across different cultures but provide closure and community support. When such traditions offer the sense of comfort sorely needed, it's clear how and why they've lasted thousands of years, helping generations during difficult times.

Our ancestors from all parts of the world have talked, written, drawn, and practiced various ideologies related to death, the afterlife, rebirth, and reincarnation. We have no solid answer, but this does not diminish the power of these thoughts.

Exercising an open mind is easier said than done, especially when you're faced with strong existential dread. Ultimately, respecting your fear involves respecting the fears of others. Everyone shares similar wonders and worries about the end. As the best of humanity shows us, we do far better when we come together to embrace the unknown than when we are left alone.

Trust me on this: You can find solace in the uncertain. You can accept the cohesion of diverse beliefs. These acts require patience and compassion. Avoid the naysayers. When people reach out and help, when they encourage debate and communication, everyone benefits.

So, let's keep the conversation going. Keep discussing, keep arguing, and keep dreaming of what's to come—for it is sure to come. When we learn to accept it, we do away with desperation and embrace a healthy fear and respect for death and what lies beyond. That's the best way to keep living.

Chapter One

The Afterlife Unveiled

Beyond the Veil of Mortality

Endings are not always bad. Most times, they're just beginnings in disguise. –Kim Harrison

The afterlife is what we believe may happen after we die. This extends to judgment, reincarnation as another person or animal, or living in the next world that could be paradise, purgatory, or hell.

Believing in the afterlife lessens the blow of impending death. It does not, however, diminish the power of death. Nothing is capable of that. But the afterlife, in all its variations, helps buffer our understanding of absolute finality in a way that does not overwhelm us completely.

We see this in tarot cards. In a deck, the Death card sometimes shows the Grim Reaper, who is often riding a white steed. It signifies the end of certain phases of life, including chances, destruction, and mortality, among others. This type of transformation encourages change for the better. When we dive deep into the nuances of tarot cultures, the death–rebirth connection is about the potential for character growth and change.

When all is said and done, we have no solid proof of any single form or interpretation of the afterlife. Yet, we need not dismiss it simply because science has not proven it. If this understanding of life after death helps humans accept the vast power of the cosmos, then it remains as important as the physics of our world.

Defining the Afterlife: A Journey Beyond

The Physical and Metaphysical

True acceptance of death is difficult. Some humans who've lived long lives and are now simply tired eagerly await it. Most of us who are busy with living, caring, learning, working, traveling, and exploring feel that every day is unfinished and that we cannot afford to die and leave things (and people) behind.

Animals are different. Have you had the incredible honor of living with dogs and cats? If you've heard of old dogs who are aware of it being their time, you may have seen or realized that they wander off to find a nice, quiet place to pass away in peace. Perhaps most animals are like them in this respect.

Memento mori is a philosophical concept that encourages us to be aware that we are all susceptible to death and must, therefore, improve our state of living in order to respect ourselves, our lives, and our endings.

Perhaps the afterlife is a realm that provides a sense of transcendence in the face of mortality. This may be the final idea that shows how vast and magnificent existence is, from the actions of an atom to the movement of celestial bodies. As a metaphysical concept, any form of life beyond death has fascinated humanity for centuries.

We dream and create stories of immortality and power because of the inescapable finality of dying. It influences us in ways we may not even realize. I consider the afterlife, in all its forms, the human interpretation of what is possible in the beyond. This must be shared and discussed, opened and studied. Does the soul really persist beyond all phases of life? I'd like to think so!

As humans who overthink, overanalyze, and extensively feel our way through life, trying to imagine a day when we simply cease to exist is outright dreadful. When this quandary was faced by people of different civilizations, faiths, and eras, they built upon these fears by coming up with possible ways to accept the end by believing it is not the absolute end.

We expend energy and time throughout life, but anything that keeps us going gives back that strength. On a higher level, people believe that this current life is just a part of our complete journey. In this way, the afterlife is a space of endless possibilities and eternal consciousness. It's where our souls transcend the limitations of the physical world and start on the journey that offers us exactly what we hope for.

Encountering Oblivion

The closest we can get to death while still living is by grieving the loss of a loved one, facing a near-death experience, undergoing a past-life-regression hypnosis, or having an out-of-body experience. While there may be more routes to achieve such a powerful experience, this book will discuss these four ways in the coming chapters.

Encountering such drastic moments is all about absorbing the overwhelming quality of death even for a short moment. When we lose a friend, family member, or pet, we are keenly aware of the void they've left behind; it's an emptiness that reminds us over and over that no matter what we do, we cannot get them back.

This lack of control can send us spiraling downward. Strong and healthy coping mechanisms can help us out of this ditch, but along this perilous journey, our perspective on death will shift. We take one step closer to truly grasping the ineffable idea of the end that will swallow the world and all of us.

This article from *Scientific American*, titled "Death, Physics and Wishful Thinking," talks of the contemplation of death from a grounded, science-based understanding, in contrast to religious ones. Josh Horgan admits that his studies in physics don't necessarily offer him comfort when it comes to accepting the looming specter of the end. In fact, people provide him with the solace he needs (2021):

> I fantasize about people reading my books after I'm gone, and I envision my son and daughter living good, fulfilling lives and possibly having children of their own. These wishful visions require civilization to continue, so I persuade myself that civilization, in spite of its manifest flaws, is pretty good and getting better. That's how I manage my terror. (para. 19)

Once we embrace the lack of control, the terror is not necessarily manageable, but it is understandable, to a degree. We get that nature cannot be controlled. We acknowledge the value of having religious ideas to help keep us on track. After all, no one really knows the destination. All we can influence is the journey.

The Cultural Mosaic: Diverse Perspectives on the Afterlife

Varying Beliefs

The world boasts various ideas of the afterlife across different cultures and religions. Some envision a paradise where the virtuous are rewarded and the wicked are punished. Others believe in the cyclical nature of existence, where souls are reborn in different forms until they achieve enlightenment. While these beliefs may differ, they all share a common thread—the belief in an existence beyond our mortal lives.

However disparate the populations of our world are, I adore the idea that people of different times and cultures have similar concerns about death and what lies beyond. These cultures have their unique takes on the afterlife in order to soothe these worries.

Here's what Dr. Desmond Biddulph had to say about Zen Buddhism's idea of life, death, and more (Wheaton, 2021):

> For many Buddhists, death isn't seen as an end but rather a continuation. We believe you go from life to life, so this can help Buddhists move away from a fear of death, and instead see it as just another part of their journey which they must take. (para. 13)

By believing in reincarnation, Dr. Biddulph explains how it's more functional to accept death. It reduces stress and addresses our lack of control in these fantastic matters.

You find similar ideologies across various religions. Hinduism talks of *moksha*, eternal salvation that breaks the cycle of rebirth. Judaism encourages living a good life to ensure a deserving afterlife based on our deeds. Atheism doesn't endorse a set standard of rules but rather emphasizes the individuality of our concerns rather than a specific spirituality. We'll cover these beliefs in detail in Chapter 8.

Coalescence

When we talk of a conglomerate afterlife, we have no objectivity to it. People from the same family who follow the same religion may still have very different ideas of life beyond death.

From the concept of Heaven and Hell in Christianity to the Day of Judgment in Islam, these diverse perspectives offer a rich and complex understanding of what awaits us beyond this life. Based on an easygoing, multichoice vantage point, we have quite a lot of options to choose from!

These varying ideas need not come into conflict but can find harmony by falling into place beside every tale. A neighbor's belief is to help themselves and not to contradict yours.

It's the promise of heavenly bliss or the possibility of reincarnation that has people absolutely besotted with the hope of more in the beyond. Some of us detest considering this a finite existence. We want more out of our one life on this planet. Perhaps we want many lives in order to explore the entire world with one soul. Or maybe we want to be assured that we have a place to go (or rather return) once it's all said and done. A home that brings no worries from this life but houses all the love and strength we desire.

I find this combination of different religions' beliefs in the afterlife to be both enlightening and thought-provoking. It reminds us that there are countless ways to perceive and interpret the mysteries of the universe. So, let's embrace this beautiful tapestry of beliefs and appreciate the diversity of human imagination when it comes to what lies beyond. Despite the lack of answers, humanity has always managed to fill the gap to the best of our ability. We've done this with each other and without, yet we've still arrived at similar points only to find others already waiting for us.

This has always been true: You are not alone in your quest.

Navigating Doubts: Addressing Questions About the Afterlife

Universal Thoughts

What happens when we die?

Whether you have a child asking you this or a Ph.D. graduate, you (and the world) cannot offer the perfect answer. People research the possibilities based on various belief systems and ancient cultures, but disparities between their conclusions ensure none of us are close to the absolute idea.

Is there a heaven and hell? Will we see the friends and family we've lost along the way? What awaits us beyond death: eternity or oblivion?

The intrigue behind these questions is beautiful and unsettling. To some, fear is certain. They dread the oncoming death beyond life. Others expect relief and freedom from mortal aches and worries. It's one thing to sugarcoat the painful truth; it's another to sidestep it altogether. Honesty involves acknowledging the importance of life, death, and all its experiences before you try to reduce its severity.

Most of us may come across death for the first time when we lose someone. Recognizing this grief is an initial step to accepting the boldness of reality. Even with the world reassuring you, the permanence of death enables us to imagine the eternity of the beyond.

When you convey this feeling to others, do you use a spiritual or religious idea? Do you approach it in an atheistic mode? The style does matter, but as long as we accept all manners of beliefs (without having to incorporate them into our own faith,) the healthy nature of doubting and questioning continues. Keep asking, and you will find that you've posed the same questions that philosophers have asked a thousand years ago. But the answers change to suit us and to soothe us.

Practicality of Doubts

Dr. Andrew Newberg is the director of research at the Marcus Institute of Integrative Health and a neuroscientist at Thomas Jefferson University and Hospital. He's known for his work on brain activity regarding religious and mystical experiences. For example, his reasoning on the tunnel of light that people with NDEs see is that their visual scope narrows when the central part of their systems begins to shut down. It leads to them perceiving light through a small gap that forms a long tunnel of darkness (Miller, 2014).

The idea that all manners of otherworldly phenomena can be explained by science is not a new one. Scientists have always believed that mystical and magical things are simple science that has not been rationalized yet.

In my opinion, the best way to broach these theories is to accept that people's doubts may last longer than what science can answer for. While it's right to accept empirical evidence, not all experiences can be categorized by numbers.

A 2013 survey connecting afterlife beliefs in the face of spousal loss studies this in depth. The paper talks about how spiritual and religious understandings of life beyond death helped people manage the loss in varying ways. From rejecting the premise to holding on to it so they can deal with the pain, the participants in the survey showed interesting patterns of strong coping mechanisms attached to their belief in the afterlife (Carr & Sharp):

> In sum, our research is consistent with an emerging literature showing that religious beliefs and practices are not universally protective in the face of all life events for all psychological outcomes ... We found that afterlife beliefs significantly predict some aspects of adjustment to loss even when we controlled for religious coping, demonstrating that the effects of afterlife beliefs on the bereavement process are independent of the effects of a traditional religious coping measure. (Section "Discussion")

When science and belief go hand-in-hand, we find the sweet spot that accommodates everyone's voices, where their worries are heard and even substantiated.

In fact, debating the concerns of what lies beyond life is not as important as finding the right debaters. People who dignify our views and whom we respect in return foster the best environment for everyone to be open about all beliefs. Even when they don't understand our ideas, they recognize our space and our voice. When we uphold this harmony toward them as well, all discussions make more sense than they did before.

Embracing the Mystery: Finding Comfort in the Unknown

Acknowledge the Secret

The great unknown is death, and the grand beyond is uncertain.

Medical professionals and firefighters are trained to work with uncertainty to assess a situation before acting. It's important for those working in emergency services to accept that a case may not provide all the information they need. These people work hard to obtain all data possible before diving in with possible solutions, even though they may never know the whole situation.

I understand where the critics come from. They excel at pointing out the holes in stories, and many are valid, to an extent. But when it comes down to it, the two choices seem to be: The afterlife is an illusion to distract us from the reality of death, and the afterlife is a hopeful endeavor that offers more than we can imagine.

It would not be right to say the world is divided into pessimists and optimists. Where are the realists and the imaginative people, the ones who dream so wild that life feels dull in comparison? What may await such souls who stay within a single body yet explore all the questions the universe holds?

There *has* to be more than what we see, hear, and taste. It's not just me wishing for this. It's also several generations before me who dreamed of stars that were once lost souls, spanning space after leaping from the horizon. The afterlife has often served a deeper purpose than just offering solace: It provides a framework for the depth of imagination and even the necessity of morality. Whether or not the afterlife exists, our belief in it inspires us to strive for purpose and make a positive impact in the world.

When it comes to events that provide no answers or solace, are you able to embrace the mystery and keep moving on? You may have to do it, and you may do so grudgingly. But it is this acceptance that liberates us from our confinement and need for all information, firsthand, right away. It allows us to focus on what we can do rather than what is missing.

We do not fare well when we fixate on emptiness or missing elements. Just as it's easy to assume a pessimistic outlook on the void beyond death, it's also easy to fall into that void and continue spiraling. This is where we recall the difference in people who understand that oblivion is a motivator to pursue their passions in life rather than succumb to the fear of uncertainty.

Cherish the Unknown

The afterlife is mostly the speculation of multiple civilizations doing their best to offer answers. The beauty lies in the way we choose to accept spiritual or humanistic perspectives. Because the afterlife is unknown, it is a cosmic buffet of possibilities. We can consume any one idea or even a combination of them.

Hear out this extract from a BBC video. The presenter brings up the ways people interpret the things we have no proof of based on beliefs (Shola, n.d.):

> There's no agreed evidence that life does continue after death. But for religious people, it's a comfort to believe that this isn't all there is; that there is an afterlife to look forward to, and that we'll see friends and family again. But many nonreligious people, like humanists, think that this life is all there is, so there's no need to be afraid of what might or might not happen after death. (1:30)

Appreciate the variety. Exercise caution when contesting others' views because you must refrain from contesting their dignity. Remember that we all mourn the same losses in very diverse ways. It's the same when we talk of death and beyond. None of us know for sure what happens when we die. When we face a truly terrifying situation, we're forced to confront our mortality without warning or preparation. NDEs push us in and out of a danger zone, and when someone miraculously escapes with their life, they gain so much more in the process.

After, the trivialities of regular life are washed in a new-found appreciation for every moment. The wake-up call to the transitory phase of living is often very alarming and effective. People with NDEs understand the value of life even better now that they've had an unwilling glimpse into death and the beyond.

We may still not have answers, but we know what we believe in, and these perspectives can change throughout our lives. And that's alright!

The journey of the afterlife is a subject that captures our attention and captivates our imaginations. We may never have concrete answers about what lies beyond this life, but as long as we keep the debate going, we keep the idea of it alive. It's a true comfort to embrace the concept of the afterlife since it enhances our journey in the world by offering overreaching potential and even eternal happiness!

Chapter Two

Unveiling the Mysteries

An In-Depth Look at Near-Death Experiences

In the first place, he can find no human words adequate to describe these unearthly episodes. He also finds that others scoff, so he stops telling other people. Still, the experience affects his life profoundly, especially his views about death and its relationship to life. –Raymond Moody

The term "near-death experience" was essentially coined by Dr. Raymond Moody, a philosopher and doctor of medicine. He understood the significance and similarities between different people who've gone through NDEs and worked on the concept for decades.

NDEs are undeniably strange. Many people describe the experience as a surreal dreamscape where the line between life and death is blurred. An NDE is the closest we can get to flitting past that boundary, and it reminds us how tissue-thin the curtain between existence and the void is.

The profound impact such an event can have on people is not to be dismissed. Nobody escapes with a stoic sensibility. We don't (and can't) just put on sunshades and walk away from an explosion behind us. Most probably, we'd be clutching our chests and panting loud, shallow breaths in total discombobulation from the experience.

Let's see how we can approach and understand NDEs and the long-term effects they have on us.

Decoding the Phenomenon: What Is a Near-Death Experience?

Near-Death Experiences Explained

As the term suggests, an NDE occurs when a person is mentally aware of a peculiar, hard-to-describe experience where they come incredibly close to dying, but by some miracle, they survive the event. This happens in a number of ways such as in severe accidents where they lose consciousness and good Samaritans perform chest compressions to get a still heart beating again.

You may have heard of patients in critical care who were medically dead for a few minutes until a doctor or a nurse resuscitated them. If the patient is not aware of it at the time, they may not have had an NDE.

The brain is an incredibly complex organ that is put to effect even when we work on mundane tasks. So, imagine the activities it performs when we're on the verge of deadly moments. When the will to survive goes into overdrive, a person visualizes or believes that they see things that the material world does not hold. In these moments, their brain runs through images and memories. Many believe they truly are seeing certain visuals that exist but are invisible to others who have not had an NDE, even if they were in the same dangerous situation.

Whatever the case, near-fatal events are powerful and intrinsic occurrences that must not be ignored because they are vital to the people who experience them.

History and Culture of Near-Death Experiences

When we look back through history, we find records of people undergoing peculiar and similar experiences to people who have brushes with death. Even with various faiths in play, people have managed to explain things using patterns of a heavenly afterlife to account for the sensations felt during the NDE.

Dr. Phillippe Charlier uncovered a medical book written in the 18th century detailing an NDE quite similar to modern-day instances. He found the account of a man suffering from a high fever who, in the process of being treated, fell unconscious momentarily (2014):

> He reported that after having lost all external sensations, he saw such a pure and extreme light that he thought he was in Heaven (literally: in the Kingdom of the Blessed). He remembered this sensation very well and affirmed that never of all his life had he had a nicer moment. Other individuals of various ages and sexes reported a very similar sensation in the same circumstances. (para. 3)

The commonalities between people across centuries who've undergone NDEs are undeniably thrilling. Many people have reported a similar blinding light and even encountering vague shapes of otherworldly beings. Various faiths explain this as evidence of the all-powerful. Science would say it's the brain slowly losing oxygen and firing away urgent messages through its overworked neurons.

Our perception of reality shifts in these near-final moments, and it's truly mind-boggling. All in all, the strangeness of NDEs captivates and intrigues us all.

Encounters at Death's Door: Credible Accounts of Near-Death Experiences

Firsthand Accounts

NDEs have long fascinated and intrigued both the scientific community and the general public. They have also had a profound impact on the individuals who have undergone them. It is through their firsthand accounts that we can begin to explore the mysteries of life and death, and perhaps gain a deeper understanding of our existence.

Gregg Nome

Nome was 24 when he nearly drowned behind a waterfall. In the process, he saw memories from his childhood, quite literally having his life flash before his eyes (Moshakis, 2021):

> Despite being trapped underwater, he felt calm and at ease. He remembered thinking that, prior to this moment, his senses must have been dulled somehow because only now could he fully understand the world, perhaps even the true meaning of the universe. Eventually, the imagery faded. Next, "There was only darkness," he said,

"and a feeling of a short pause, like something was about to happen." (para. 1)

Judith Ford

Judith Ford was five when she slipped from a pier and fell into deep water. She was instantly surrounded by gentle imagery and calming sensations rather than the terror of drowning (Ford, 2023):

> One minute I'm in the bright, hot sunshine, and the next minute I'm somewhere else. It's cool here, and the light around me is green, green everywhere. I'm slowly, gently sinking. There are sunbeams sliding down all around me and long thin green plants dancing in front of me. A fish goes by. I like being here. It's soft and quiet ... I remember the magic of suddenly finding myself in a totally unfamiliar, beautiful world. I wasn't afraid until I saw my dad's fear. (para. 8 & 12)

We may have encountered our fair share of skeptics who dismiss NDEs as mere hallucinations or tricks of the mind. But that doesn't negate the numerous accounts of people who are high-ranking professionals in their respective fields.

In fact, Ford's experience contributed to the life she
lives, seeing as how she has written and published several
award-winning books. Ford has also consistently researched
the psychological and spiritual effects of grief, NDEs, and
brushes with death.

Eben Alexander

These firsthand experiences have not only changed the lives
of those who have undergone them but have also had a profound impact on their approach to life in the aftermath. Another such professional is Dr. Alexander, a practiced neurosurgeon who fell into a week-long coma after suffering a
severe E. coli infection of the brain. He writes in his book,
Proof of Heaven, (2012):

> My experience showed me that the death of the
> body and the brain are not the end of conscious-
> ness, that human experience continues beyond
> the grave. More important, it continues under
> the gaze of a God who loves and cares about each
> of us and about where the universe itself and all
> the beings within it are ultimately going. The
> place I went was real. Real in a way that makes the
> life we're living here and now completely dream-
> like by comparison. (p. 9)

The good doctor was adamant that he had not been in his body during the coma and had existed in a large cosmos beyond anything Earth or humanity could have produced. His encounters with magnanimous sensations of love cemented the idea that he had an ethereal glimpse into the afterlife.

In an interview with ABC News, Alexander spoke of an angel who conveyed messages of love to him with silent eyes. As it turned out, he later found a photo of his biological sister who he'd never met or known before. Alexander instantly identified her as an otherworldly angel. "I looked up at that picture on my dresser that I had just got and I knew who my guardian angel was on the butterfly wing ... It is the most profound experience I've ever had in this life" (2012, para. 17).

Dr. Alexander documented much of his experience and other lessons from life in *Proof of Heaven*. He talks of visiting a tranquil and beautiful valley. Otherworldly beings of light interacted with a great, spiritual entity that he calls Om or God. Alexander recalls it as a place of unconditional and unlimited love, revealing that the valley was true life, and his existence on Earth was a dull version of the possibilities of the afterlife.

His account of the experience is doubly intriguing because Alexander is a neurosurgeon with years of experience and expertise regarding brain function in different states of health. While he was skeptical of such out-of-body and NDEs before the coma, this memorable event took centerstage. The doctor was aware that his brain had been compromised during the coma.

The vivid visual of the valley of divine entities forever changed his concept of life, death, and beyond. Alexander truly believes he was in a realm of light and love, connected with all the entities on a level that didn't even require speaking. The experience left him in a state of revelation and opened his mind to the possibility of a beautiful but uncertain afterlife. His recollection brings the spotlight onto NDEs, their validity, and the relationship between science (that which can be proven) and spirituality (that which is trusted).

Interpretations

Extraordinary brushes with death not only challenge the understanding of consciousness but also allow people to develop different approaches to life.

These professionals who have had credible NDEs have undoubtedly changed the fields in which they work. We will read up on Bruce Greyson, who developed the Greyson Criteria to determine when a close call with death results in a strong NDE. When educated and compassionate people accept new and wild theories with the intent to decode them without judgment, that's when science truly helps people during these indescribable times.

It's all about opening up new avenues of research and sparking important conversations about consciousness and the human experience. This transformative power allows us to broaden our minds to avoid prejudiced notions to find the truth or the path closest to the truth.

Responses

NDEs are not solely about the mystical moments but are also about the following days and years when people try to interpret what they saw. How do their friends and family react to such a bewildering event? If you've had one, how did your loved ones respond to your strange experience? Have you had the honor of hearing a trusted person's NDE?

The responses deeply affect the attitude someone has to their own experiences. Focus on the credibility of the experiencer's emotions rather than your interpretation of their dream-slash-experience. It's normal to feel afraid, grateful, or confused. It also helps to suggest professional help if it's required. Alternatively, simply be there to listen and provide comfort. Remember, responding with compassion and understanding can make a significant difference in someone's recovery and healing process.

Bridging the Gap: Scientific Research on Near-Death Experiences

Body and Mind

Have you heard of the paradoxical undressing? It's a term for people with hypothermia who have the inexplicable need to take off their clothes when they're freezing. They report feeling hot and sweaty when caught outdoors in snowstorms or stuck high up on snowy mountains.

It's truly bizarre to imagine people on the brink of a cold death having the urge to undress to cool off. However, this phenomenon was explained by focusing on people with extreme hypothermia. During this stage, their bodies automatically contract their blood vessels to preserve warm blood flow to the major organs and away from extremities like the limbs (Lallanilla, 2013). This causes a hot flash that makes disoriented, freezing people feel as though they're sweating and burning up.

True, this is more a bug than a feature, but it shows how the body is a fascinating network of systems. We have the instinct for survival that pushes us toward help and away from unquestionable danger no matter what. Most times, these are involuntary actions enabled by our incredible physical bodies that are capable of things we only discover in times of crisis.

Science Talk

A well-known survey poll was conducted in 1992 by Gallup that revealed that about 5% of the U.S. population back then had personal experiences with NDEs (Jeff, n. d.). That's a whopping 13 million citizens in the country. While the study wasn't based on certain age groups, the results showed that both children and adults had had NDEs.

The Epoch Times published an article consolidating various NDE-related surveys done on Americans, one done on Germans, and one done on Australians, with laymen and medical professionals participating. It spoke of the significant percentage of people who experienced similarities in their NDEs across countries and professions. "Near-death experiences (NDEs) are reported by an estimated 200,000 Americans a year, and studies around the world suggest NDEs are a common human experience" (MacIsaac, 2023).

International Association for Near-Death Studies

The International Association for Near-Death Studies (IANDS) is an organization dedicated to the study of NDEs. With a mission to promote understanding and research in this intriguing field, it's at the forefront of exploring the mysteries of what happens when we come close to death.

Founded in 1981, IANDS has grown into a global community of researchers, medical professionals, and individuals who have experienced NDEs themselves. Their collective efforts have led to groundbreaking discoveries and a deeper understanding of this phenomenon. By providing a platform for sharing personal accounts, conducting scientific studies, and organizing conferences, IANDS has become a hub for those seeking answers and validation.

Dr. John Audette and a few other pioneering researchers, namely Raymond Moody and Bruce Greyson, founded the Association for the Scientific Study of Near-Death Phenomena in 1978, which was later renamed IANDS. Audette was known for his steadfast dedication to the studies and work conducted by the organization, and he spent years of his life building off the works of Moody and Elisabeth Kübler-Ross (Moody, 2015).

Greyson Scale

Dr. C. Bruce Greyson, a leading researcher in the NDE field, has published numerous studies that highlight profound psychological changes in survivors. Greyson's NDE scale was developed to measure the depth of people's NDEs to develop a more uniform approach to studying the data.

His criteria comprise 16 questions that a layperson can answer and assess for themselves. Further discussions are best conducted with expert analysis, but as a first step, Greyson's questionnaire ranges from queries about sensations of time dilation, joy and harmony, vivid out-of-body experiences, and encountering peculiar beings, among others.

The questions are divided into four sections: cognitive, affective, paranormal, and transcendental (Greyson, 1983). If the person can rate their experience on a scale from 0 to 2 for every question, they can figure out if the NDE they had fits the scale's criteria. People with a score of above 7 (out of 32) are categorized as having had an NDE.

Remember the 18th-century medical book uncovered by Dr. Phillippe Charlier (Section "History and Culture of NDEs")? The archeologist tested the book's account of an NDE against Greyson's scale and concluded that the patient in the book scored 12 out of 32 (Gholipour, 2014).

Greyson's scale has been used and cited hundreds of times over the years and has been able to gain close to conclusive evidence that NDEs have a certain pattern, regardless of time period, faith, and the cause of the event.

Monitoring Brain Activity

When working with NDEs from a purely scientific perspective, people have tried to conduct surveys and polls to gather data on brain and body activity during NDEs or just before death.

Dr. Sam Parnia is a director of research on cardiopulmonary resuscitation. He has encountered cases of patients having out-of-body experiences with relative authenticity. Nasia Colebrooke's article, "Is There Life After Death? This Doctor Thinks So," shows how Parnia recalls the situation of a man who lost consciousness, stopped breathing, and "had an out-of-body experience where he watched himself be resuscitated. He was able to provide an accurate and verifiable description of the room, the nurses, and the doctors and what they were doing" (2019, para. 4).

Parnia calls this "conscious awareness." This state lasted in the patient for 3–5 minutes during which the professionals found no brain activity.

Tracking brain activity prior to death is an ongoing area of research. Scientists have discovered that in the final moments of life, the brain can remain active and engaged to a certain degree, even if the person does not show regular signs of response.

This *Smithsonian* magazine article highlights a remarkable collection of medical insights that confirm gamma wave action in the brain prior to death in patients who'd suffered cardiac arrests (Sullivan, 2023):

> Researchers saw intense signals in an area of the brain that can be active when people have out-of-body experiences or dreams. "If this part of the brain lights up, that means the patient is seeing something, can hear something, and they

might feel sensations out of the body," Borjigin
tells Issam Ahmed of the Agence France-Presse.
(para. 8)

People may worry about feeling stuck in a body that is
unresponsive at the very end of life. However, the research
shows hope that the brain sometimes engages in lucid imagination that takes the patient into a dreamscape where pain
and anxiety are never near. Again, concrete evidence cannot
be garnered since we're a long way off from recording such
results. We can always have hope that the end is a gentle
curtain to pass through rather than a brick wall.

Dispelling Doubts: Addressing Skepticism About Near-Death Experiences

Conflicting Proof

You will find as much trust and research in NDEs as skeptics
find data proving the opposite.

Consider the views of Dr. Adrian Owen. He's an acclaimed
doctor who has conducted deep research on the human
brain for several years. His combination of neuropsycholog-
ical studies with direct neuroimaging of brains has unveiled
incredible scientific results, which allow his lab to refine the
detection and diagnosis of brain injuries in future patients.

From his results, he has deduced that the mind and the brain are interlinked. One cannot exist without the other. When it comes to NDEs, Owen finds these cases to be strong examples of the final images and hallucinations that the brain is capable of when it runs low on oxygen or has suffered trauma. "The brain is the organ that produces consciousness, full stop. If you take that organ away or kill that organ or that organ dies, you cannot be conscious" (Colebrooke, 2019, para. 9).

Near-Death Experiences Versus Hallucinations

We see this when NDEs are compared with hallucinations, vivid and rushed alike. While a state of altered perception is common ground for both, the similarities end here. People who've experienced both NDEs and hallucinations can distinguish the impact of each.

People who've gone through NDEs report a range of vivid sensations, including feelings of peace, seeing a bright light, and even encountering deceased loved ones. These experiences are often accompanied by a sense of detachment from the physical body and a heightened awareness of the person's surroundings. In contrast, most hallucinations are typically characterized by distorted perceptions and sensory experiences not entirely based on reality.

NDEs are even consistent, to a degree, across different cultures and belief systems. People from various backgrounds and religions have reported similar themes and elements in their NDEs, suggesting a universality to these phenomena. On the other hand, hallucinations can vary greatly from person to person and are often influenced by individual factors such as mental health, medication, sleep deprivation, nature, and nurturing styles.

Hallucinations are typically fleeting experiences that can startle and terrify people but do not leave the type of profound impact that is found in people who have had NDEs. The most obvious answer to this disparity is that not all hallucinations are caused by deadly circumstances, but all NDEs are a result of shocking events. Folks who experience them often exude a greater sense of purpose and a shift in priorities, mostly toward a positive angle.

Anecdotal Evidence

Hallucinations can be reproduced in labs for testing purposes. Strong medication, when mixed with powerful sedatives, can cause lucid imagery and spike brain activity. NDEs are, by nature, impossible to recreate in a controlled setting. They are categorized as anecdotal evidence since these moments are derived from and documented thanks to personal experience only. It is not the kind of scientific finding that can be verified.

That's one of the contentions of this field. NDEs cannot be monitored by any kind of equipment. We can track heart rate and blood pressure during surgeries and resuscitations.

Even when people are on the verge of passing away in ICUs or monitored locations, brain activity tells us a lot. The fact is, when brain function slows and stops, the mind is inactive. But we know from accounts that people have had NDEs even when brain activity seemed to be low to nil. Case in point, Dr. Eben Alexander was examined, and it was confirmed by medical professionals and his family that he was simply not aware during his coma. Alexander himself agrees that he wasn't in his body during his NDE.

We have no unbiased empirical data to support an NDEs occurrence. Instead of taking this as a defeat, we can use it to further our view on NDEs. It is not interpersonal, yet somehow fantastical and even universal to an extent. If it cannot be proved, it cannot be disproved either.

Fostering Understanding: Near-Death Experiences and Their Impact on Our Perception of Death

The best part of considering NDEs is finding out how closed- or open-minded you are. True NDEs have the power to completely reshape our understanding of life and death. They challenge beliefs and open up a realm of possibilities that we may have never considered before.

One of the most striking aspects of NDEs is the sensory consistency of the reported elements. People from different cultures and backgrounds often describe similar encounters, such as moving through a tunnel, encountering a bright light, or feeling a sense of peace and love.

As mentioned before, one of the best potential results of surviving an NDE (alongside surviving!) is having a new-found appreciation for life. The transformative effects of open-mindedness and a healthy respect for death lead to positive changes in behavior and outlook. People strive to live more wholly and authentically. In this way, NDEs can catalyze personal growth and spiritual development.

From the accounts we've seen, we understand that the most valuable things are the qualities of love, compassion, and hope in a space where prejudice and hate have no place. When translating that into life and earthly existence, perhaps these visuals are lessons for us to realize that the people in our lives hold high priority. Our gentle happiness, not necessarily frugal but not needlessly lavish either, does as well.

NDEs can revolutionize our understanding of death. These firsthand accounts of the afterlife are filled with raw sensations and passionate beliefs that we are not facing a heartless void at the end but rather a hopeful afterlife. True, we don't know the specifics. We may never know them. However, the concept of believing in a vague idea is based on how that idea makes us feel:

- Does it fill us with serenity or dread?

- Is the idea impeding or supporting human rights?

- Is it a personal justification that does not require anyone else's input?

I believe that as long as our understanding of the spirituality and realism of NDEs does not infringe on other people's dignity, it stays true. Perhaps the real trials occur when we're forced to acknowledge the eerie and even eldritch quality of it all. This circles back to the immense lack of answers. There's only so much we can yell at the sky before our voices grow hoarse. The odds of receiving answers that soothe us are rather low.

That's how NDEs can actually help us! We face the limits of our mortality, and it reshapes our perspective on life. Suddenly, the value of everything mundane and regular increases tenfold. Material pleasures take second place to the real connections we foster in life, nurtured by this absolute wake-up call of a lifetime.

But you can also see it as an opportunity to reflect on the meaning of life and what comes next. Change your decisions, make new goals, discover silly hobbies, stick to old targets, revive a childhood dream, or do a complete overhaul. Life isn't about going through the years and making sure you hit every social milestone for extra points. It's about so much more than we can fathom. It's a philosophical journey with a dash of mystery thrown in for good measure. Who doesn't like a good mystery show? And you get to be the main character!

This is what transformative moments can do for people, not just for the individual. Together, it leads to a deeper appreciation for life and a greater sense of spiritual connection.

Chapter Three

Unearthing the Spiritual Gold

Lessons From Near-Death Experiences

I imagine death so much it feels more like a memory. Is this where it gets me, on my feet, several feet ahead of me? I see it coming; do I run or fire my gun or let it be? There is no beat, no melody. –Lin-Manuel Miranda

Thinking back on a near-death experience may remind you of the overwhelming and floating sensations you were accosted with during the event. In fact, people routinely revisit the memory in order to recall the absolute absence of negativity in that divine space of serenity.

We've spoken about how such transcendent experiences lead to drastic changes in people's lives, vis-à-vis attitudes, decisions, and lifestyles. Now, we discuss in detail how to best learn the lessons from an NDE.

Done right, it's a positive cycle of returns where you can keep reaping the benefits of your NDE by making radical changes in the way you live. So, let's take a look and go about finding the innate sense of peace that we really deserve!

The Common Thread: Love and Compassion in Near-Death Experiences

Documented accounts of NDEs share the idea that the afterlife is filled with love and acceptance in all the forms that matter to the individual experiencing the event. Near-death moments themselves are horrifying and distressing, but the out-of-body or visual experiences that people have turn out gentle or revelatory. They are not painful by any measure.

This is reminiscent of Em James Arnold, who had a cardiac arrest and was completely unconscious during the 90-minute resuscitation process that included 9 defibrillator shocks. Arnold has had gender dysphoria since the age of 3, which is important to this account (Tamkins, 2023):

> During the near-death experience, the cardiac arrest survivor—who was assigned male at birth and now prefers they/them pronouns—had a profound and life-changing memory. Arnold re-

members traveling feet-first over an expanse of
water, floating on what seemed to be a stone-like
surface. Overhead was an endless sky, and Arnold
felt completely safe, free of fear, and neither male
nor female. (Section "There Was No Gender")

It is supernaturally awesome that Arnold's experience affirmed their identity while providing them a new lease on
life.

In the 1970s, Betty Eadie's childhood bout of whooping
cough and pneumonia had pushed her to the brink of death
when the doctors and nurses realized she'd even stopped
breathing. Yet Eadie had heard them declare her dead and
even explain to her parents that she was gone.

While this happened, she was in a different place. In fact,
she was in the arms of a man with a white beard that fascinated her. She explains this in her book, *Embraced by the Light*
(2002):

I felt perfectly calm and happy with him. He
gently rocked me, cradling me in his arms, and
although I didn't know who he was, I never
wanted to leave him ... This experience would be
mine to cherish as an oasis of love throughout
my young life. The memory has never changed,
and each time I remember it, I get a sense of the

calmness and happiness I had in his arms. (pp. 7
& 8)

This was not the only NDE she had, and it proved the
existence of greatness in the beyond.

NDEs seem to offer more than what we may assume at
first. Survivors experience encouragement and love not only
for others but toward themselves. The events add hope for
people to build on their character and relationships.

Life Review: The Mirror of Our Actions

In Reality

You'll have heard of flashbacks occurring during NDEs.
They're absolutely possible, seeing as how your memories
may mix with visions. For example, at 55, Connie Fuller's
heart stopped due to bradycardia. She was administered CPR
so strong that the nurse broke some of her ribs. Fuller recalls
no pain from the episode, just sensations, mainly hearing her
husband's voice from 40 years ago. "We started dating when
I was 14, he was 16 ... He sounded like that little 16-year-old
boy. That was the voice that I heard" (Tamkins, 2023, Section
"I Knew I Could Not Leave Them").

Fuller believes that the young voice of her husband helped
her wake up. The flashback builds on the theory that the phe-

nomenon of an NDE offers a glimpse into the relationship between the brain, the mind, and how memories are stored.

On a much stronger level, some people see longer visuals of past events summed up in a phrase called "life review." Such types of flashbacks are sometimes vivid recollections of the past, often occurring in a nonlinear and fragmented manner.

The experiences of Dannion Brinkley substantiate this. He's a former U.S. Marine who has had multiple NDEs. In 1975, he was hit by a bolt of lightning! Brinkley had an out-of-body experience for a full 28 minutes. "His consciousness traveled through a tunnel, where he encountered a spiritual being of light and underwent a grueling replay of his entire life. And then, in a flash, he says he was back in his severely injured body" (Knapp, 2021).

Brinkley's life reviews involved him witnessing thousands of schoolyard fights he had been involved in. It left him feeling unfulfilled and yearning to be useful to others rather than being the same kind of person he had been as a kid.

He is now a steadfast helper of people, and he keeps heavy topics light but dedicated. He runs the Twilight Brigade, a nonprofit organization whose volunteers help ease the end-of-life transition for veterans and elders nationwide.

In Fiction

The concept of life reviews has enamored people for ages. We see this even in popular culture where characters in fiction have flashbacks before their possible death scenes.

It's demonstrated in the internationally known play, *Hamilton*, where the character of Alexander Hamilton belts out a soliloquy for the audience just before he is shot. His monologue is about all the things he'd done in life and if it had ever been enough. Hamilton speaks of all the people he sees on the other side, before finally telling the vision of his still-alive wife to "take your time. I'll see you on the other side" (Kail, 2020).

In Essence

Art imitates life. A life review transports people back to significant moments in their lives, sometimes allowing them to relive and re-experience them with astonishing clarity. It challenges our conventional understanding of memory, suggesting that the review may not be a straightforward process but rather a complex web of interwoven experiences. Flashbacks in NDEs can be emotionally intense, activating a range of feelings veering from joy and nostalgia to regret and sorrow.

In essence, a life review is the clearest and deepest mirror you can hold up to yourself. You see not your face but everything you are, your soul, thoughts, decisions, actions, and emotions. The truth is often laid out so bare that it shocks you out of the humility of wondering what others will think and have you going, "So this is how I truly am?"

Rate yourself out of five. How many stars will you give to the life you've lived? What changes do you yearn to make?

The Interconnectedness of All Beings

Through NDEs, we find an undeniable string that connects every experiencer and weaves a fabric holding us all on a single line of thought. What if the truth is just as simple as we are shown? What if the afterlife truly is a space of peace and love for all?

NDEs reported across cultures and belief systems suggest this universality despite differences in faiths. While I don't believe in a one-size-fits-all scenario, I am accepting of an answer that helps everyone in different ways. We have a range of experiences, and people feel and think differently all the time. This is what believers say when we show how diverse backgrounds do not divide us but rather help us add to the flavor of this spiritual interconnectedness.

The Lancet Study

The 2001 study by Dr. Pirn van Lommel and his team focused on 344 patients from the Netherlands who had suffered cardiac arrests. Of them, 62 patients reported NDEs. This collective forms 18% of the group, and their experiences were categorized based on variables of age, gender, and type of NDE event, among others.

The team observed that out-of-body perceptions and purely NDE experiences happen despite low to nil heart rate and brain function (Lommel et al., 2001):

> How could a clear consciousness outside one's body be experienced at the moment that the brain no longer functions during a period of clinical death with flat EEG ... Another theory holds that NDE might be a changing state of consciousness (transcendence), in which identity, cognition, and emotion function independently from the unconscious body but retain the possibility of nonsensory perception. (Section "Discussion")

The study also found that visually impaired persons described true visual perception during their NDEs. It was clear that such experiences challenge the current scientific understanding of the human mind. To pursue the field would mean to broaden our views and accept that the answers may just startle us over and over again.

Interconnections

Despite the low percentage of NDE occurrences, it's still mind-blowing to have such happenstance across the world. The consistency within this low number is remarkable in itself when you take into account that people have experienced NDEs throughout history. Without documentation, we cannot assume much, but we can be sure such cases have happened based on the sheer number of people who have lived on this planet since before the Common Era.

These experiences provide compelling evidence for the spiritual connection that exists between all individuals. It's up to you to accept this deeper spirituality that indicates that we're not alone in this world. We have the chance to explore the interconnectedness of our spiritual selves. Embracing this reality leads to a more compassionate and connected world. We're more than social creatures—our connections exist in the messy, invisible fabric of the world. NDEs' transformative effects can awaken this dormant awareness within people, reminding them of the importance of acknowledging truth, love, and connections.

Once we recognize the illusion of divisions, we understand the grand power of what unites us. It seems NDEs are ways to catch sight of the possibilities of everything that connects strangers on a level devoid of violence and hatred. It's about understanding where you stand in life, where you can go from here, and how we can do it together.

The Transformative Power of Near-Death Experiences

Lighthouse in a Storm

These intense encounters with the threshold of mortality can alter the person having an NDE's perspective on life. The sheer ferocity of an NDE often leaves individuals with a sense of awe and wonder as they witness the mysteries of the universe.

Howard Storm is an art professor turned pastor who experienced an NDE that showed him unnamed beings threatening to take him to hell in pieces before he called out the name of Christ in desperation. Speaking just a few sentences of the Gospel sent them away immediately.

The Standard-Times published an article that talks of Storm's harrowing NDE, which culminated in a ray of light approaching him slowly (Rodrigues, 2011):

> This was a living being approximately 8 feet tall and surrounded by an oval of radiance. The brilliant intensity of the light penetrated his body. Ecstasy swept away the agony. Tangible hands

and arms gently embraced him and lifted him up.
(para. 18)

Previously atheistic, Storm responded to this encounter
by becoming a devout Christian. He's now Pastor Storm of
Zion United Church of Christ based in Cincinnati. His 2000
book *My Descent Into Death and the Message of Love Which
Brought Me Back* details his NDE and the lessons he's learned
about life.

Dr. Rajiv Parti shares a similar instance of changing his
approach to his faith based on his transformative awakening
from an NDE. Following a severe case of sepsis, Parti recalls
floating above his body, traveling to hell, navigating through
a time tunnel, reaching Heaven, and meeting a few deceased
relatives.

He describes his experience of hell in an interview with
Lynn Fishman (2016):

> There was fire, and there I could hear people
> crying and wailing, and I was being pulled—a
> bushfire source. I was shocked and realized, "This
> is a hellish area." My first reaction was: "Why
> am I here? What have I done wrong?" While I
> was asking this question and asking for help, my
> father showed up ... I had so far lived a very selfish
> life. It was all about me, and it was "How can I get

ahead? How can I achieve this success?" It was all about me ... When I was in the tunnel area with my father, I had a review of my life. (9:02–12:51)

His impromptu *Divine Comedy*-esque journey left him enlightened and incredibly unfulfilled with his lavish lifestyle. In fact, Dr. Parti changed careers and began volunteering, helping out in various projects to shift his focus to healing not just his physical body but his mind and consciousness as well.

Such character transformation that urges people to change careers, faiths, and their entire brand of living is difficult to believe but absolutely possible. We love to find such stories and such people who have managed to pick themselves up after such a dangerous, hopeless time in their lives.

Creating Hopeful Stories

We constantly see such transformations repeated in the stories we tell, such as *It's a Wonderful Life*. This is a movie in which George Bailey, at the brink of depression and ready to make a dangerous decision, is found by an angel who helps him climb out of that pit and embrace the brilliance of life.

Puss in Boots: The Last Wish shows the jaunty protagonist—who was previously careless about wasting his life—facing an expert bounty hunter who's never missed a mark. Puss sees his life flash before his eyes in two separate scenes (Crawford et al., 2022).

Spoiler alert! It turns out the bounty hunter is actually the personification of Death, who is after Puss because of his disregard for life. In the end, our hero gains a healthy respect for life and for fighting for his right to live well.

This movie for children encapsulates the terror and beauty of living despite the specter of death looming over everyone. The titular character recalls the best moments of his life and the experiences shared with his trusted friends, and he understands the value of living to the fullest even in the face of death.

Pain and Power

It is through these experiences that some people find solace, purpose, and a renewed zest for life. We've seen this with Howard Storm, Dr. Rajiv Parti, and Dannion Brinkley. They came out of NDEs with a heightened realization of the beauty and interconnectedness of all life.

Of course, an NDE itself comes with a host of trauma and pain, and to suggest that people must have brushes with death is uncaringly cruel. This book focuses on the potential good that comes out of NDEs, flipping the narrative of "death is bad." Death is neutral, horrifyingly so. Life is what we make it, good, bad, and ugly.

When we see people wake up from harrowing events with a sense of courage and the will to change, it's heartening. This is what I wish to discuss. This is what has captured my attention and what I believe has caught yours as well.

The sudden change can pull the rug out from under your feet. When you learn to stand back up again, you can develop compassion for the fragility of life rather than constantly fearing the end. In this way, NDEs can improve the quality of life for people who've lived through them and also positively impact the world through these people.

Applying Spiritual Lessons to Daily Life

Spiritual Lens

Changing your views doesn't mean you've lost the argument. It means you've gained knowledge and are adapting to the truth you've now learned.

Allow yourself the leeway to backtrack and find new lessons in the gap you've left. This tactical retreat is valuable for any kind of life. It's where you can accept things that never made sense before. You can dismiss ideas that you know will never help you. You can learn so much more when you give yourself the space to hold more thoughts and perspectives than before.

Spiritual lessons range from heavily religious behavior to mildly mystical sentiments. Perhaps it is not for all, but it is certainly for people searching for solutions and who are ready to devour all the answers they find.

This American Psychological Association report connects the occurrence and frequency of spiritual experiences occurring for near-death experiencers daily, based on the recollection of the event and its intensity (Khanna & Greyson, 2014):

> Frequency of daily spiritual experience after the close brush with death was significantly higher for those participants who reported NDEs than for those who did not. In addition, among those who did have NDEs, depth of NDE as measured by continuous NDE Scale score was positively associated with the frequency of daily spiritual experience since the close brush with death. (Section "Discussion")

It looks pretty straightforward. Survivors register their spirituality in life and all around them when they pay close attention to what the world has to offer. These brushes with death enabled them to slow down and smell the roses, to appreciate what was right in front of them rather than constantly sprinting to score a distant goal.

The study acknowledges that people of various faiths will experience their spirituality in different ways. This understanding bolsters the links between such experiences and NDEs. It proves there is a spiritual melting pot filled with how people interpret the world and its events based on their singular (but expanded) perspectives.

Practicality

A portion of the world will say there is nothing practical about NDEs. Another portion will jump on the bandwagon and eagerly point out all the lessons you can learn. It's up to you to choose what you want to gain out of the event that acts as a checkpoint in your life.

We've mentioned Betty Eadie's journey in her book *Embraced by the Light*. She locks in the understanding that her family had everything they needed to live a fulfilling life, and yet it took them a while to really get things started. Following her hysterectomy surgery, she fell ill and experienced her mind-bending NDE.

She writes that even as she moved through the motions of her consciousness, watching herself with a third-person view and traveling into a tunnel, she was "filled with the desire to move on with my own life and to experience all that awaited me" (Eadie, 1992, p. 35). Even then, she was steadfast in understanding that death wasn't the end but merely a precursor to another form of living.

Eadie goes on to say her meeting with the brilliant entity of light was in fact Christ the Savior. He greeted her but admitted that it was not yet her time (1992):

> My time would come when my mission, my purpose, my meaning in this life was accomplished. I had a reason for existing on Earth ... his love and acceptance for me never wavered. My thoughts raced on: "Is this Jesus, God, the being I feared all my life? He is nothing like what I had thought. He is filled with love." (pp. 42 & 43)

Eadie understood this rejection to mean she had a purpose on Earth to live in a specific way. And more than that, she had no need to fear God since all he had was love for her.

Her lessons from this NDE are intriguing ideas that she lives by to this day. She spreads her message of love and healing to people, emphasizing the need to do away with fear of God and rather just focus on compassion and gratitude. She believes that a person's faith must not scare them into doing the right thing but must bolster their soul at all times.

What is your take on finding useful advice from inexplicable events? When you have the time to really deconstruct your layered emotions, you'll find the safe spots and the brave spots where you can dance to your heart's content!

Incorporating Life Lessons

When we are faced with our mortality, we are forced to confront our priorities, re-evaluate our choices, and gain a new perspective on life. It's how these experiences serve as wake-up calls, jolting us out of complacency and pushing us to make positive changes.

This transformative power of NDEs should not be underestimated. They ignite a fire within us, propelling us toward personal growth and a more fulfilling existence. In fact, a remarkable quality of people surviving NDEs is their ability to extinguish their terror of the end.

I probably seem like a broken record at this point, but this is so brilliant to consider. NDEs don't just show us what could be waiting for us in the afterlife. They also offer us chances to change our lives for the better. It's the best deal!

We have not proved the existence of a soul. Where might it reside? In the heart with your emotions or in the brain with your memories? In the gut with your instincts or in the spine with your courage? Or is the soul spread all over the body like a sheet of silk under your skin or wrapped around your bones?

We can't answer that concretely, but we love to say yes, yes, YES! In that vein, we say yes to an afterlife as shown by the beauty of the visions in NDEs.

Chapter Four

Beyond the Physicality

Out-Of-Body Experiences

You can't stay with your body even for a minute. You wander off in thoughts, imaginations and dreams. So you are certainly not the body. To know who you are, ask yourself this: Are you coming to the same body after each trip outside?
–Shunya

Yes, out-of-body experiences (OBEs) are different from near-death experiences. NDEs can be OBEs, but OBEs can occur outside of near-fatal situations. It's like how all thumbs are fingers but not all fingers are thumbs.

We've had cases of induced OBEs thanks to strong medication (monitored or not). People have reported feeling detached from their bodies in a way where the world still exists, but they are the ones that have changed. Such a detachment happens temporarily and with or without a time-dilation effect—where the experiencer feels like too much or not enough time passes during the event.

Understanding Uncommonality: What Is an Out-Of-Body Experience?

An OBE is the vivid sensation of somebody's consciousness floating outside their physical body. This is a rare occurrence but can happen during events of heightened awareness (e.g. meditation), while being severely drugged (e.g. surgeries), and during NDEs.

The experiencer senses a startling separation of the soul from the body. People attach their consciousness to this soul and recognize the body as a vessel that has carried them from birth to this moment in life. In many cases, experiencers feel that they hover above the body and see themselves and the world from this elevated position.

History of Out-Of-Body Experiences

The term "out-of-body experiences" was first recorded in 1943 by George Tyrrell in his book, *Apparitions*. It's been used for circumstances involving astral projection and spirit walking, as called by various cultures. Astral walking, or projection, involves a person's consciousness leaving their physical body and exploring the world beyond.

OBEs have gained attention through the work of researchers and individuals who have claimed to have had such experiences. A notable figure is Robert Monroe, who popularized the term "out-of-body experience" through his books and research. He founded the Monroe Institute, which focuses on exploring and understanding the phenomenon.

The institute's website brings on a helpful idea of how OBEs can be achieved by focused meditation and trance-inducing techniques. Monroe's studies emphasize the necessity of being able to look beyond the physical life to appreciate everything in the world, not just the material aspects. The meditation strategies were about self-actualization to gain insight into the body, mind, and life itself using out-of-body trances as a tool to learn more.

Out-Of-Body Experience Occurrences

OBEs can occur in other situations. Intense spiritual practices can induce a sense of separation between consciousness and the physical self. Strong dissociation episodes can lead to uncontrolled OBEs. Certain hallucinogenic substances have been known to cause similar experiences.

According to a recent American Psychology Association paper, following significant OBEs, people reported feeling motivated to pursue their previously feared life goals, having a better idea of peace and how to achieve it, being able to prioritize their relationships better, and even having a lesser fear of death (Shaw et al., 2023):

> These findings suggest that OBEs in healthy individuals could be an uncommon but natural part of life's transformative events, unfolding as part of the development of the human psyche and offering potential benefits to the experiencer, which may be accessible to those that seek to induce the OBE intentionally through practice. (Section "Conclusion")

This re-evaluation of the participants' place in the world allows us to see how OBEs can embolden people and that these experiences are natural indicators of exceptional events in a person's life.

Such situations offer a glimpse into the mysteries of the human mind and its relation to the world. They challenge our understanding of consciousness and the nature of reality. OBEs are a shadow of the vastness of the mind and its potential for exploration. Such events continue to captivate and intrigue, opening doors to new possibilities and expanding our understanding of the world around us.

Exploring the World: Credible Accounts

People around the world find themselves in the unique position of experiencing something beyond the physical realm. They go on to explore and understand the complexities of life in general.

The ability to recall specific details and accurately describe their surroundings during these OBEs adds weight to their claims. It's not something experiencers dismiss lightly but rather something they embrace as a valuable learning experience.

Pam Reynolds

In 1991, 35-year-old Reynolds was admitted for surgery to address the large aneurysm in her brain. Her survival expectation was low, but the team of more than 20 professionals did their best and succeeded. When Pam Reynolds woke up, she could tell exactly what had happened during the operation, watched the instruments used, heard the conversations between doctors and nurses, and witnessed the state of her body during the whole session.

Dr. Michael Sabom's book, *Light and Death: One Doctor's Fascinating Account of Near-Death Experiences*, chronicled interviews conducted with people, one of them being

Reynolds, who has perhaps the most famous accounting of her OBE (1998):

> The further out of my body I got, the more clear the tone became. I had the impression it was like a road, a frequency that you go on ... I remember seeing several things in the operating room when I was looking down. It was the most aware that I think that I have ever been in my entire life. (n.p.)

Beyond the surgery, Reynolds also drifted away from the room and into an afterlife scene where she met some of her deceased relatives. She had the distinct sense that there were other entities following her journey. They told her to be careful of where she went in case she got too far from her physical body.

This vivid and detailed account invited conversation and controversy. But there was no denying that Reynolds knew exactly what had happened in the operating room because she'd watched the medical team the whole time. Her case remains notable since it provides evidence of how the consciousness functions without brain activity.

Anita Moorjani

Moorjani was in a coma in 2006 after suffering from cancer for years before. She experienced a strong OBE where her consciousness moved away from her body for a significant amount of time (2013):

> It felt as though I had a 360-degree peripheral vision. I could see everything happening all around my body. But not just in the room where my body was, but even beyond. And it was as if I had expanded out of my body. I was aware of my physical body, I could see it, lying there on that hospital bed, but I was no longer attached to that body. It felt as though I could be everywhere at the same time. (3:16)

She was in Hong Kong during this experience but was aware of her brother boarding a flight in India. In the unnamed space, she even met her father and a close friend, both of whom had passed away. They guided her on the journey where she saw others in ways that couldn't have been possible with human limitations.

Susan Blackmore

Blackmore was a first-year student at Oxford when she had an OBE while high on hashish with her friends. In *Psychology Today*, she writes about her experience backed with the brain functions that operated during her OBE (Blackmore, 2019):

My auditory cortex was similarly hyperactive, producing random low-frequency repetitive sounds that drowned out the music. It sounded to me like the pounding of horses' hooves. I was galloping fast down the tunnel towards the light. When Kevin asked, "Where are you, Sue?" I was brought up short. I tried to picture my own body and where it really was, but my prefrontal cortex was deactivated as the brain hovered on the edge of sleep. (pp. 6 & 7)

Now, Blackmore works on consciousness during OBEs, NDEs, meditation, and spirituality. She writes on these topics and more in her books, academic papers, and magazines. Her unique perspective on the mysteries of OBEs makes her writing all the more compelling to add to the growing list of unexplained experiences.

Whether you believe in the metaphysical or not, it is difficult to deny the impact these experiences have had on people and the potential they hold for expanding our understanding of the human experience.

Overarching Insights

Reynolds, Moorjani, and Blackmore reported their OBEs with startling detail despite nearly slipping into death. Their miraculous recoveries and recollection of the events show

how the consciousness is capable of more than what the brain purports. Gaining fascinating glimpses into the world beyond our physical bodies is a serious rush and often changes our perspectives on life and death.

Many cases of OBEs happen during NDEs such as cardiac arrests, strokes, comas, severe infections with high fever, and the like. As with the two women discussed here, it's up to the patients to interpret the OBEs as they wish. When the events are seen as inspirational catalysts, the patients make it their ultimate goal to pursue happiness in all aspects of their lives. This includes career, relationships, community involvement, and personal growth.

To make drastic choices and change our lives is no small feat. We see the effects motivated by a decreased fear of death that allows people to show gratitude to the world and kindness to themselves when going through difficult changes.

These accounts challenge our conventional understanding of the human experience. They push us to consider the possibility of a deeper connection between the self and the universe.

Deep Dive: Scientific Research

OBEs have long fascinated scientists and researchers. Numerous scientific studies have been conducted to explore this intriguing phenomenon. These studies aim to understand the nature of OBEs, their potential causes, and their impact on people.

A study conducted by Dr. Olaf Blanke and his team used virtual reality technology to induce OBEs in healthy individuals. By manipulating sensory input, they created the illusion that participants were outside their physical bodies. This groundbreaking research offered valuable insight into the neural mechanisms underlying such experiences (Blanke et al., 2004).

While there is still much to learn, these studies have contributed to our understanding of the human mind and consciousness. Below, I look to more research that can open new avenues to answers. Let's keep discussions open about the boundaries of human perception.

Spontaneous Out-Of-Body Experiences

The exact cause of any kind of OBE is rather mysterious. They can occur in a range of cases, from traumatic events to deep meditative trances.

OBEs are a dissociation of the mind from the physical body. During moments of extreme stress or trauma, the brain may enter a state of heightened awareness, allowing the person to perceive their surroundings from a different vantage point. This detachment from the physical body can create a sense of freedom and exploration, leading to a profound and transformative experience.

Researcher Nerea Herrero and her team reported on OBEs and the behavioral techniques of the patients surveyed. The work suggests that these experiences can occur spontaneously and under various circumstances. This challenges the belief that OBEs are solely associated with NDEs. "OBEs are linked with self-consciousness, which depends on multiple neurocognitive mechanisms and processes, including the experience that our body belongs to us, embodiment sensation, and being aware of the present moment" (Herrero et al., 2022, Section "Introduction").

While the scientific community may still be divided on the exact mechanisms behind OBEs, the journey to reach these answers is forever illuminating. Whether or not they're a result of altered states of consciousness, these experiences offer a unique perspective on the nature of our existence.

Induced Out-Of-Body Experiences

OBEs can be brought about by meditation, lucid dreaming, and safe medications. By entering a deep meditative state, people can safely transcend the limitations of the physical body and explore different realms of existence.

"There appears to be a possible link between meditation practice and the occurrence of OBEs, with half of the study participants engaging with a meditation practice" (Shaw et al., 2023). This study observes a similar finding to various papers on the subject, further showing how a fraction of the population chooses to engage in OBEs to find clarity and learn more about themselves and the world around them.

Such experiments not only provide valuable insights into the nature of perception and self-awareness but also offer potential applications in fields such as psychology and neuroscience. I applaud the efforts of scientists who are pushing the boundaries of our understanding.

One study on OBEs was conducted with one group of induced OBEs being compared with a group of people who'd had spontaneous OBEs (Herrero et al., 2022):

> We further analyze the differences between specific emotions experienced during OBE episodes. We found that the OBE (induced) group had a significantly lower frequency of "Fear" emotion as well as a significantly higher frequency of "Happiness", "Love", "Hope", and "Euphoria" than the OBE (spontaneous) group. (Section "Type of Emotions Associated")

While the study did not find notable differences between the groups for emotions of curiosity, anger, anxiety, and indifference, among others, the paper itself offers us nuanced data that OBEs affect people differently based on reason and individuality.

Induced OBEs have become a fascinating avenue of scientific research. By using various techniques such as virtual reality, sensory deprivation, and electrical stimulation, researchers can explore the mysteries of the human mind and consciousness.

It's refreshing to see such innovative approaches in the pursuit of knowledge. It's not just about satiating our curiosity; it's about understanding how these experiences truly affect and change people around the world every day.

Revelation on Out-Of-Body Experiences

Aside from NDEs and meditation, situations of lucid dreaming, drug highs, and general anesthesia have been known to cause sudden and spontaneous episodes of OBEs.

These experiences provide people with a sense of freedom and liberation. No longer bound by the limitations of their physical bodies, people can explore new realms of existence. This expanded consciousness provides a fresh outlook on life, helping them break free from old patterns and beliefs that may be holding them back.

This was stated in a recent study by Jade Shaw and her team. "This experience should also be assessed by its potential fruits rather than by its roots alone. The meaning people make from these experiences, and the ways in which they can impact people's lives in the wake of them, remains under-studied" (Shaw et al., 2023).

By transcending the physical plane, people may gain a more nuanced idea of the universe and their place within it. This newfound wisdom inspires personal growth and a greater sense of purpose. With more potential research on the horizon, we can truly understand how the transformative effects are just as valuable to the overall study of OBEs.

Chapter Five

Unraveling the Threads of Transformation

How Near-Death Experiences Change Lives

I knew you were there with me. You know I felt that I had been travelling in a long cave which was full of darkness. Suddenly, you had come from nowhere and held my hands and brought me out from the cave. Were you with me in this journey? –Neelam Saxena Chandra

The appreciation and farsightedness gained from near-death experiences can have a profound impact on our lives. By embracing the present moment, prioritizing personal connections, and re-evaluating our priorities, we live a more purposeful existence.

Self-transformation is all about consciously changing our habits, attitudes, and perspectives to realize our own potential. It's not necessarily being the best versions of ourselves but recognizing how to simply be better than we were before. NDEs help people find that the lives they have been living could be better if they just make a few adjustments to their choices and approach.

We see this in many stories of transformative experiences. We've covered this in brief in Chapter 3, so let's discuss the significance of self-transformation and the surreal advantages we, and everyone around us, can gain from these lessons.

Rethinking Life Through the Lens of Death

Ingredients for Empathy

NDEs are all about revealing incredible information to us. We may witness life reviews, have an out-of-body experience, discover the backstage secrets of the afterlife, speak to our deceased loved ones, or experience all of these things.

Transformative goals are never easy. We've read about people who've changed careers and made grand life decisions because those avenues were important to them. You must figure out what's crucial to you. It differs from person to person. For some, their families are the most important thing, for others, it's their jobs or personal interests. However you want to embrace change, you must focus on realistic goals that bring you true joy. Where possible, aim to change your life based on the following aspects.

Personal Goals

Setting your own goals to bring fulfillment to your life is crucial. Self-awareness is your friend here, and it pays to embrace the change that happens when you make your own choices, decide for yourself, and work on your personal journey without relying on others to make your decisions for you.

By all means, take advice from trusted people. But at the end of the day, are you choosing for yourself or to satisfy others? It doesn't help anyone to be a people-pleaser. When you step back and re-evaluate your past choices, do you discover something new? How many of your choices were based on what others wanted of you?

In most cases, we do things for people because we care about them, and they need our help. It's not always so clear-cut, and you may find yourself wondering if your personal goals were ever truly yours. If not, it always helps to take extra time to figure out where you're going and how you're going to get there.

When you put your foot down, you draw strong boundaries to get people to respect you. This, in turn, helps you respect yourself. It's how you grow to be a self-assured person in the face of trials.

Improved Relationships

When we improve ourselves, we raise the standards of the company we seek. Our platonic, romantic, familial, and professional peers can stay in our realm of interest because there must be an equal amount of give and take. These relationships build and influence us to the same extent that we work on them.

Our self-transformation helps us develop a better understanding of ourselves that in turn brings clarity to our relationships. We cultivate our listening and communicating skills while our personality takes on a more compassionate edge. By involving such fulfilling interactions, we subconsciously draw people with similar empathetic drives that match our energy. They understand the kind of relationships we want to build and are more accepting of our limits and preferences.

In the same way, people who have unhealthy connections with us may demand more or lash out when we don't agree like we used to. It's a turning point in those relationships, where we either give them an ultimatum to change their ways, help them out to save the relationship, or cut them out of our lives. It's never an easy choice, but we must recognize that these choices are truly available to us, and each one is unique with its pros and cons.

In the end, we can navigate life's challenges with a group of wonderful friends and families who have our backs. This is the type of support system that truly matters in life—the people who do not judge or step out of line to insult others behind their backs. It's a journey to get to this point, but this is a true test of character, and it fosters healthier connections in ways that may seem miraculous.

Better Resilience

Bad things will happen as sure as good things do. We cannot control everything in our world. We experience far too many events that are way beyond our control, and it's vital to realize that and accept that we cannot influence everything.

We can, however, choose how to respond to the less-than-desirable events. Pick your battles. Do you want to stand for certain things until the end of time? At what point do you draw the line? Where are your boundaries set? Does everyone know what your boundaries are?

These are questions you must try to answer to have a better understanding of what makes you tick and how you want to improve. You will face terrible, horrible, no good, very bad days. But will you be able to take time off and work on the issues or your self-care? Developing this kind of resilience in order to face terrible news is one of the best things you can do for yourself, especially in an age where we are constantly aware of setbacks, failures, rejections, and horrible information from all over the world.

Living your life to the fullest involves dealing with the unexpected and the icky stuff. When you're able to confront issues with a mature and wholesome perspective, you can understand the complexities of a problem, and you will also be able to find potential solutions thanks to your out-of-the-box thinking.

Memento Mori

Death is a part of life. We've heard this across time and space in books and movies and from older and wiser people. In Latin, memento mori means "remember that you will die." It's a way of saying, "Yes, the end will come for us all, but that makes life all the more valuable."

You won't be surprised to know that people who've had a significant brush with death—and realized that they'd been that close—now treasure their mundane moments a lot more. This translates to NDEs as well, where exploring a possible afterlife scenario is a stark reminder of how precious it is to live.

In Kenneth Ring's publication, *Heading Toward Omega*, he examined 14 cases of NDEs and found that the experiencers had varying senses of heightened spirituality following their event (1984). This was shown through a new appreciation for life, empathy for others, a search for a more fulfilled life, and a feeling that they were closer to God or an equal omnipotent power of the universe.

It's important to note that this lessening of fear was mostly about lower anxiety rather than lower respect. Death still commands a hold over them, as it does for everyone. But rather than feeling constrained by the worries about their final destination, people were emboldened by the vast potential of life and their paths.

We find this in the well-known book, *The Crossover Experience,* which talks of different NDE accounts and how people make their way through life with inner peace to build resilience (Kadagian et al., 2022):

> I learned, after the NDE, that I have a choice all the time as to how I want to structure my experience, and I can follow any path I want. It doesn't matter once we cross over to the other side. It simply does not count for ANYTHING... ever. So why choose a harsh life experience? We don't have to ... We use far too much energy trying to live our earthly lives in a way we believe constitutes happiness, but it is such an illusion. I experienced the ease of living without money, status, time, etc. (n.p.)

It's all about the strength of our self-awareness. When we understand the power of our intentions and decisions, we make the active choice to learn new ideas, forge connections, and build healthier habits. Life is no longer a structured routine full of specific milestones for us to follow. Rather, it's an open road spreading out in all directions, and if we decide to frolic through the sunflowers, then that works as well!

Life-Changing Stories: Personal Transformations Post-Near-Death Experiences

Changes in Living After Near-Death Experiences

Many of us live thriftily in order to secure a good future while some splurge on the present with no regard for others. It's easy to say that we must live in the moment with due regard. NDE survivors make it an art form.

David Ditchfield

In 2020, Ditchfield's coat was caught in the doors of a train, and he was pulled along for the ride before falling onto the tracks. He partially lost his arm and dipped into the afterlife for a few brief moments. Despite the harrowing event, Ditchfield knew that he was too calm. He recalled seeing a beautiful place where he felt love and support.

In the aftermath, he went on to change some aspects of his life in significant ways. He picked up painting to try and create a visual of what he'd seen during his NDE. He has gone on to live a healthier life with a more active and supportive mentality toward the world (Taylor, 2020):

> I feel like I'm living in different dimensions rather than just one. I'm much more sensitive and can pick up on the energy of places and people. It has made my life so much more interesting ... I have a lot more appreciation for nature, and the world seems a beautiful place. I love watching animals and insects, watching the seasons change. (Section "The Long-Term Effects")

He talks about how he's changed his perspective on relationships as well. He's far more accepting of the nuances and differences among people. Instead of heading straight for anger or disappointment, he's more forgiving of the world and has learned to be supportive of everyone.

Howard Storm

We've mentioned Storm, the art professor turned pastor, in Chapter 3. In 1985, he suffered a stomach perforation and collapsed, experiencing an NDE that nearly dragged him to hell before he ascended into brilliant light.

Storm documents his transformation and will to live a fulfilling life in his book, *My Descent Into Death* (2005):

> Prior to June 1, 1985, I lived my life in the pursuit of happiness. There were fleeting moments of sensual or ego gratification ... I was mildly depressed much of the time. Happiness comes and goes ... Ever since June 1, 1985, I have had joy in my heart. I have had moments of the full range of emotions, but the joy stays constant. Real joy is independent of the events in our life. Joy is being in an intimate relationship with God. (p. 94)

Howard Storm lives not as a God-fearing man but as one who is fully aware that the Almighty has nothing but love for everyone. Every day is a gift, and it is one that Storm lives, content in the knowledge that his decisions are all geared toward living the best life possible with inner peace and joy rather than material successes.

Unintentional Changes

P.M.H. Atwater is an NDE survivor and a long-time researcher of near-death studies. She has written multiple books on topics regarding her NDEs and her research on many patients with similar experiences.

Based on her studies, people have reported the following material changes in their bodies and their styles of living. "Stress easier to handle, lower blood pressure, increased
intelligence, clustered thinking (as opposed to sequential),
charismatic, quicker assimilation, increased allergies of various kinds ... latent talents surface ... a hunger for knowledge"
(Williams, 2019, section "Physiological Aftereffects").

These transformations were unexplained in many cases.
You'll have heard of people knocking their heads and waking
up speaking fluent German despite never visiting Germany or
taking language classes. NDEs have a strong influence on the
psyche, and people come out the other side with impeccable
knowledge of life that changes every aspect of them, even
physical tastes, in some cases.

Intentional Choices

NDE survivors may emerge from their encounters with a
renewed sense of purpose and a determination to make the
most out of their lives. They understand the fragility of existence and are motivated to live each day to the fullest. Experiencers often report a shift in priorities, placing more em-
phasis on relationships, personal growth, and pursuing their
passions. Their experiences serve as a wake-up call, reminding
them to seize the day and embrace all that life has to offer.

Their choices reflect this. NDErs develop the drive to make
positive changes in their lives and the lives of others. They

pick up new hobbies or restart abandoned ones. They connect with others without second-guessing themselves and often show less anxiety in social situations than the average person.

Such people report a heightened appreciation for the simple joys of life, such as the warmth of the sun on their skin or the taste of a delicious meal. They become advocates for living authentically and passionately, inspiring those around them to do the same. Their stories serve as a powerful reminder that life is a precious gift, and it is up to each individual to make the most of it.

Despite the challenges they face, NDE survivors exhibit remarkable resilience and a zest for life. This is reminiscent of Anita Moorjani, David Ditchfield, and Howard Storm, who live with a renewed passion for the present moment. They have been to the edge of existence and returned with a beautiful sense of purpose. NDE survivors serve as a testament to the human spirit's ability to overcome adversity and find meaning in even the most difficult circumstances. Their stories are a source of inspiration and a reminder to us all to live each day with intention and gratitude.

Applying Insights From Near-Death Experiences to Everyday Life

Science-Backed Impact

Dr. Jeffrey Long is a medical professional and practicing radiology oncologist who contributes to NDE research as well. His articles on the Near-Death Experience Research Facility (NDERF) site are known for their clarity with numerical data and his books on NDEs span a collection of authentic accounts as well as the scientific take behind the events.

He estimates that there are about 774 cases of NDEs every day in the United States, a total made up of all cases that go reported and unreported. As explained in this NDERF article, (Long, n.d.):

> In spite of these limitations, this estimate of number of NDEs occurring per day is probably accurate within an order of magnitude. I am not aware of any other methodology that has been used to estimate the number of NDEs that occur in a given time period. The goal of this article is not to definitively answer this question, but to encourage further consideration of this interesting question. (para. 7)

Long, as do many others in the field, often invigorates more study and data search on the matter of NDEs because the work we have is never enough. Our goal is not to just achieve survey results but to prove how consistent discussion truly improves everyone's recognition of NDEs and to understand the value of such an event.

Spiritual Insight

An NDE can serve as a wake-up call, forcing individuals to re-evaluate their priorities and make significant changes. Personal growth is often accelerated as a result of a newfound appreciation for life and a desire to live more authentically. These experiences are incredibly valuable and can lead to profound positive changes.

Death is an inevitable and truly anxiety-inducing part of life. NDEs have pushed people to refocus on life and confront these fears head-on. One way to do this is by embracing the present moment and making the most of each day.

NDEs have never been for the faint of heart. But coming back from one offers the person a colossal chance to shed their worries and truly meet life's challenges directly. Many often emerge with the desire to explore a new level of spirituality. This requires a willingness to question everything they thought they knew and a commitment to facing their deepest fears. This can be done with the following steps:

1. **Open your mind**. Embrace the possibility that

there's more to this existence than meets the eye.

2. **Self-reflect**. After an NDE, you've had a taste of what lies beyond this mortal coil. Take the time to think about your experience. What did you learn? What did you fear? What do you want to change? That's what you start working on.

3. **Recognize the fear.** Embracing spiritual awakening after an NDE means facing your deepest fears head-on. It means stepping out of your comfort zone and venturing into the unknown. Yeah, that's not exactly a walk in the park. But when you're willing to confront your fears, you might just find that they hold the key to your spiritual growth.

When you're ready to dive into the depths of your soul and face your darkest fears, go for it! By setting these goals, pursuing passions, and cherishing relationships, we can shift our focus from the fear of death to the joy of living. Additionally, practicing mindfulness and gratitude can help us appreciate the beauty and wonder of life, further alleviating needless worries about death. By realizing life and all its possibilities, we can confront the anxieties of death with a sense of purpose and fulfillment.

Practical Advice

One of the board members of the International Association for Near-Death Studies, Robert Mays, had this to say (Kaleem, 2014):

> The stories vary, though they usually involve something like being in a place of all knowledge or a city of light, seeing a tunnel, heaven, or angels, being out of your body and watching yourself or a very fast life review before people are told or have the feeling they need to "come back" to life. The theory is that consciousness can separate from the body itself. (p. 18)

What can we glean from this knowledge along with the information we've been working with for the past few chapters?

- First off, let's embrace Mays's theory that consciousness is not limited to our physical bodies. NDEs consistently reveal the existence of a greater reality beyond our earthly existence. By acknowledging this, we can expand our perspective and open ourselves to new possibilities.

- Secondly, prioritize love and compassion in interactions. Relationships often mold us into the people we desire to be. So, it's important to fuel the kind of relationships we want. NDEs often emphasize the importance of love as the ultimate force in the universe. By practicing kindness and empathy toward others, we can create a more harmonious lifestyle that involves the right kind of people in our lives.

- Thirdly, cultivate a sense of gratitude for life's blessings. If you find yourself taking things for granted, you will be left adrift when they suddenly go missing. NDEs often leave individuals with a deep appreciation for the simple joys of everyday existence. By actively acknowledging and expressing gratitude for the abundance around us, we enhance our overall well-being.

Accepting these ideas into our daily lives requires a shift in mindset and a commitment to personal growth. It's how we create a more meaningful and fulfilling existence. So, let's take these lessons to heart and make the most of each day, knowing that life is a precious gift to be cherished!

Chapter Six

Reincarnation

Unearthing Past Lives and Beyond

I could well imagine that I might have lived in former centuries and there encountered questions I was not yet able to answer; that I had to be born again because I had not fulfilled the task that was given to me. –Carl Jung

Is reincarnation really in the scope of near-death experiences, or are we moving way beyond science and the metaphysical, you may ask? I respond with this: We dream about rebirth and dance with the theories of multiple lives and living after death, but we have no empirical proof about reincarnation.

Well, science is the proof of everything our ancestors dreamed of. And we won't find concrete data on reincarnation or prove anything unless we talk about it.

Packed in this chapter are the explanations and accounts of people who have demonstrated unexplained traits learned from previous lives. More than that, I offer my session on past life regression, a personal account of the life I've lived before that explains so much of what happens in my present.

Demystifying Reincarnation: An Introduction

Reincarnation is the idea that our consciousness, or soul, will live on after our physical death and be reborn as someone new in our next life on Earth. This is a concept spouted in religions and various cultures but also talked about in various philosophy circles.

I bring up reincarnation here because, aside from judgment and oblivion, rebirth is something a significant portion of humans think about. You might not find the same peace and solace from this topic as others do, but I assure you, there's an integral idea of give-and-take preserved in rebirth.

Religions and Cultures

Samsara

Hinduism works on the cycle of life, *samsara*. This is a term that refers to birth, life, death, and rebirth as a cycle that everyone goes through. Samsara is about how people are essentially stuck living on Earth and must figure out how to escape from the cycle to attain liberation, called moksha.

Buddhism also regards samsara as an unstoppable cycle of life and death that cannot be broken itself, but it can be escaped to attain enlightenment or Nirvana. This faith's teachings are geared toward achieving escapement—freedom.

Jainism follows this same idea that our lives are trapped in this cycle of rebirth. Observing the rules of ahimsa, a path of nonviolence, helps people break out of the cycle successfully (National Geographic Society, 2023).

Sikhism names this escape *mukti*. Until it is achieved, people are doomed to be reborn to face the consequences of their actions from their previous lives. When they're able to leave and end the cycle of reincarnation, they reunite with God.

Free Will

Judaism has a specific sect, Kabbalah, that observes the idea of reincarnation as a distinct part of living. It emphasizes the meaning of individuality and the allowance for every person to choose to reincarnate to complete their responsibilities (Tilles, n.d.).

Metempsychosis

Here's a fancy word of the day for you! Metempsychosis is the transmigration of a human soul from one body to another in the interval between death and new life.

Ancient Greek mythology has this in abundance, what with divine gods, goddesses, and demigods running the place. The poet, Pindar, finds the concept of rebirth suitable for grand mythical figures of mythology. He is quoted by Plato (5th century B.C.E):

> Persephone shall accept requital for ancient wrong, the souls of these she restores in the ninth year to the upper sun again; from them arise glorious kings and men of splendid might and surpassing wisdom, and for all remaining time are they called holy heroes amongst mankind. (Meno, 81b)

Pindar states here how some souls are guaranteed another round of life based on their deeds on Earth while others are not allowed reincarnation.

Ancient Egyptian mythology also favors the idea of rebirth, as written by Herodotus (5th century B.C.E):

The Egyptians were the first who maintained the following doctrine, too, that the human soul is immortal, and at the death of the body enters into some other living thing then coming to birth; and after passing through all creatures of land, sea, and air, it enters once more into a human body at birth, a cycle which it completes in three thousand years. (History 2.123.2)

Throughout history, it seems a significant portion of the population did believe in reincarnation, even if solely to find comfort from the finality of death. Perhaps it was heartening to accept that the soul was immortal while the body was not.

New Age Spirituality

Conceptualized a few decades ago, the New Age belief accepts an all-powerful divinity that exists throughout the universe and even within ourselves. Unlike the concept of a deity called God, this is more akin to an omega-level power that exists everywhere. The movement focuses on the spiritual self since divinity is notably within the consciousness while also accepting the idea of partially divine entities (angels) who can channel awesome energy.

According to a Gospel Coalition article on New-Age concepts, some Christians do believe in this form of spirituality, one that's not fully spouted by Christian commandments

(Carter, 2018). They, along with people of other faiths, understand and accept the idea of reincarnation since it helps dull the finality of death in our world.

This is because they find a clear positivity concerning reincarnation. People see it as a second chance at life to try and continue the work they are doing now. There's certainly a comfort in the notion that our souls may have multiple chances to learn, grow, and evolve. This adds a layer of depth and meaning to our existence, making each life experience a stepping stone toward enlightenment.

Karma and Kismet

Aside from merely sounding awesome, karma and kismet are terms that give many of us quite a lot of meaning. Karma is Sanskrit for an action and the reaction to it (cause and effect). In Hinduism and Buddhism, it is the understanding that a person who's lived a wholesome life with good deeds to their name will be reborn in a new life with good luck and prosperity. Similarly, a person who has been selfish and evil to their neighbors and nature will have the misfortune of being reborn in a difficult life with many trials.

Right away, you may see the concerns here. Have you faced an issue in life and wondered what you'd done to deserve it? Personally, I don't think it's right to be punished for something I can't even remember. It's truly cruel to tell someone sick or injured that they deserve their suffering on a cosmic level.

This is where kismet steps in. It's Turkish for fate or destiny. Kismet talks of fate as an unfathomable force that powers our choices and consequences according to the will of the world. We have no control over the results, only on our decisions. I suppose kismet is a more palatable option to the anxieties caused by karma. But together, they are an unstoppable duo, the love child of humanity's creativity and belief.

In essence, reincarnation is either the consequence of your actions in a previous life (karma) or the result of fate playing dice with your life and choices (kismet). It's interesting how some faiths see rebirth as an earthly problem and not a reward. It all depends on how much stock you put into your karma and kismet.

Personal Narratives: Stories of Past Lives

Dr. Ian Stevenson is a psychiatrist from the University of Virginia. He's spent years working on specific cases of reincarnation in various countries. Here's an interview of Stevenson by Dr. Kirti S. Rawat (Bowman & Bowman, 1995):

> I think reincarnation offers a better explanation
> for some unusual behavior that occurs very early
> in life and often persists throughout life. This is
> behavior that is unusual in the person's family.

He could not imitate it from other members of
the family or inherit it from them. (para. 6)

The interview was done after the publication of Stevenson's book *Twenty Cases Suggestive of Reincarnation*. His
work is titled "suggestive" because, despite the extensive research conducted by dedicated professionals, we cannot have
perfectly substantiated proof of rebirth by any measure of
concrete data. We do have some incredible accounts that are
similar, though, and these must be discussed fully and will-
ingly if we are to gain any ground.

A more recent work by Dr. Stevenson is *Where Reincarnation and Biology Intersect*, published in 1997. It covers even
more stories from across the world of children recalling specific memories from their past lives and giving details that
nobody else could have known. He writes this about unexplained and irrational fears of young children (1997):

Phobias, nearly always related to the mode of
death in the previous life, occur in about 35% of
the cases. A child remembering a life that ended
in drowning may be afraid of being immersed in
water; one who remembers a life that ended in
shooting may show a phobia of guns and loud
noises. If the death occurred during a vehicular
accident, the subject may have a phobia of auto-

mobiles, buses, and trucks. (Section "Introduction")

According to Dr. Stevenson, traits of intense likes and dis-
likes tend to manifest in kids before they are able to verbally
communicate. This is based on the fact that before being
able to speak to their family, they have not had the experience of learning about most fears and passions. This opens
the possibility of them remembering the strongest memories
from their past lives. But he does admit that such phobias and
-philias fade to an extent as children grow.

Understanding stories of past lives is a fascinating journey
into the unknown. It does not help to dismiss them outright
since that would be a disservice to the richness of human
imagination and the potential for deeper understanding. It's
always worth exploring these stories with an open mind.

Phobias are most connected to the way the children had
died. In fact, stories of reincarnation often include children
retelling their deaths. Some of the following stories involve
people who died prematurely in their past lives.

Solving His Murder

A 3-year-old boy in the Golan Heights (name not given) fig-
ured out that, in his past life, he was actually killed by somebody. His family took him through various villagers before he
found the murderer (Mehta, 2014):

Suddenly, the boy walked up to a man and said, "Aren't you ... (Eli [Lasch] forgot the name)?" The man answered yes. Then the boy said, "I used to be your neighbor. We had a fight and you killed me with an axe." Eli told me how the man had suddenly gone white as a sheet. The three-year-old boy then said, "I even know where he buried my body." (para. 7)

He led the authorities to a site where they did find a body in the earth. It was the paranormal end to a gruesome, unsolved missing case. This is documented by Trutz Hardo in *Children Who Have Lived Before: Reincarnation Today*, published in 2005.

Recognizing Her Son

Despite growing up in 1930s New Delhi, India, 4-year-old Shanti was adamant that her home was in Mathura (a city nearly 90 miles away), where she had a husband and child. She spent years trying to convey the urgency of this to her parents and teachers (Wehrstein, 2022):

To test the girl, Kedar Nath pretended to be his brother, Babu Ram Chaubey, and sought facts from her that only he and Lugdi had known.

With him, he brought Lugdi's son Naunita Lal. Shanti Devi was not deceived. She pointed out that Kedar Nath still had the moustache and facial birthmark that she had described to her parents. She threw her arms around Naunita Lal and cried as she never had before, saying that her soul recognized his soul. (Section "First Contacts With Prior Family")

The story shocked the local population. It was acknowledged that Shanti Devi was truly Lugdi Chaubey in her past life. The child knew far too many details of the family to not have some afterlife mysticism at play here. Her story went international thanks to Sture Lönnerstrand, a Swedish researcher, who wrote about her account in his 1998 book, *I Have Lived Before: The True Story of the Reincarnation of Shanti Devi*.

Overall, these stories are ultimately subjective experiences. Each person's interpretation and understanding of their past lives are unique to them. Rather than seeking concrete proof or validation, it's more valuable to approach these stories as a means of self-reflection and personal growth.

While accounts of past lives may be met with skepticism, some of them even having been debunked, the ones that stand the test of time offer a window into the mysteries of our existence. By considering their historical context and embracing their subjective nature, we gain a deeper understanding of ourselves and the world around us.

Hollywood Memories

Ryan Hammons was four when he conveyed to his mother that he used to be an actor on Broadway and in Hollywood. After a year of trying to convince her about his past life, Cyndi Hammons found Dr. Jim Tucker, who is a child psychiatrist and a professor of psychiatry at the University of Virginia. As the narrative goes, he got in touch with an expert in archiving old movies (Taylor, 2021):

> A film archivist (employed by a TV production company who made a documentary about Ryan) identified the man Ryan said was "me" as Marty Martyn, a dancer, actor, and agent who died in 1964. When Tucker visited Ryan and his parents, Ryan was asked to pick out photos of people and places that related to Marty Martyn, which he did successfully. (Section "The Case of Ryan Hammons")

Ryan ended up relaying 55 verified statements about his life as Marty Martyn without ever reading up about the man or his family. In fact, since Martyn died in 1964 and was a relatively small-time actor, he wasn't all that documented online.

Birthmark of Charcoal

Anurak was born in Thailand in 1969 to parents who had lost a son three years before. Anurak's deceased brother was Chatchewan, who drowned in a nearby klong (canal). At Chatchewan's cremation, a family member marked his elbow with charcoal. Anurak has a birthmark on the same arm with a similar shape (Stevenson, 1997):

> When Anurak became able to speak, he made a few statements referring to the life of Chatchewan. He spontaneously recognized and called by his nickname a young man known to Chatchewan. He searched for and found Chatchewan's Boy Scout uniform in a wardrobe that had other clothes in it. Anurak had a marked phobia of water. (Section "The Prediction of Birthmarks")

Beyond the birthmark resembling the charcoal spot, the family truly believed Anurak was their boy who had returned to them for a second life. His recollection of memories from moments that stood out in Chatchewan's life was undeniable to them. This account is documented in Stevenson's book, *Where Reincarnation and Biology Intersect*.

Past-Life Regression: A Therapeutic Approach

Past-life regression (PLR) is a fascinating therapeutic technique that has gained popularity in recent years. It's about guiding individuals into a relaxed state where they can access memories from past lives, similar to hypnosis. This process is known to help people gain insight into their current life challenges and patterns. I've even experienced it myself, and the results explain so much of my current life!

Past to the Present: The Same Negativity

I've always been curious about the past, mine in particular. It's a natural thought process to wonder how my situation in a previous life contributed to my current state of affairs. I spent a good number of years trying to work on my relationship with my mother to no avail. It seemed like we'd had this incompatibility between us, which I suppose many daughters can relate to, but I've been particularly hurt by this negative energy.

It doesn't help that my radar for clocking red flags in terms of relationships with men has been down for a long time. It's true that people in terrible long-term relationships often go back to similar situations because that's their source of familiarity. It takes serious intervention and introspection to break that cycle of self-harm and toxic environments.

I chose to try a set of hypnosis sessions to check out my PLR concepts. It's not like I was on the fence about it. I truly believed any kind of help was good help. The sessions were fruitful, and I gained an insight into my personality and life that many other avenues could not offer.

My sessions helped me recall memories that I had not experienced in this life. This was more than an active, visual imagining. These were thoughts I had had but not as the current me. I saw horrible imagery of a dead man hanging in an old building; his eyes were still open. It dawned on me that I was the one who caused this since he'd hurt me for years. It was an image that has stuck with me because I noticed details that would not fit current times. The man's clothes were in an older style, not at all consistent with the 21st century. I myself felt less than real in this memory. I was more of a spirit-based observer. I didn't even have feet during this recollection!

This transfer of negative energy into my current life was so real to me. My ex and I had hurt each other so badly in our previous lives that the present carried the same toxicity.

The hypnosis therapist gently guided me further back into the past. I saw a girl carrying a long knife, and I instantly knew she was me. More memories came to me. I saw myself living in what was perhaps an orphanage with several girls younger than me. I saw the people who adopted this past version of me, the same people who are my parents in this life.

I recognize a lack of love between all of us in this earlier life. It's disheartening and enlightening at the same time.

It's the same cycle of negativity from that first memory of the man. Just as my ex and I found no peace in our relationship, my parents and I had the same subconscious misgivings carried over from before. We were doomed to repeat the cycle had we not chosen to intervene and get help.

The session revealed more memories, and I awoke with low positivity. Yet, I gained clarity from the truth, however horrible it was. All the terrible events from my past were clouding my present. They were obstacles in my way to happiness. I spent a long time working on myself, practicing self-love and compassion for the world and myself. It was a painstaking process, but I am in a better place now and am working on my relationships.

This was the introspection I needed to break out of that cycle of negativity that my past life threatened for my present. I firmly believe these therapy techniques help all of us in some way or another but only if we wholeheartedly believe in them.

Answers to the Unexplainable

PLR sessions have been known to provide valuable insights for many. They offer a fresh perspective on our current life issues. By tapping into past-life memories, we can gain a deeper understanding of the root causes of our challenges. This reveal is incredibly empowering, as it allows us to make conscious choices and break free from recurring patterns, case in point, me!

We can find emotional healing and closure in a successful therapy session. People with irrational fears (phobias) may want more information on why they feel fear toward certain things and events when they may never even have encountered them before. By revisiting past life experiences, individuals have the opportunity to find such answers and even release any unresolved emotions or traumas that affect their present lives.

Some folks also find PLR sessions to be a source of personal growth and spiritual exploration. They allow individuals to connect with their higher selves and tap into their innate wisdom. They also offer a deeper understanding of a person's purpose and a greater sense of fulfillment in life.

PLR subscribes to the idea that reincarnation is real and that our soul is constant through the centuries that pass by. We absorb the energies from every life and carry them into the next. It's up to us how we can focus on our strengths to be better versions of ourselves.

If you really think about it, it's amazing how our souls truly vibe across time and space.

The Scientific Scrutiny: Reincarnation Under the Lens of Science

Research and Randomness

The belief that, after death, the soul is reborn in a new body has long been a subject of scientific skepticism around the world. While many cultures and religions embrace the concept, the scientific community remains divided. Some argue that there is insufficient evidence to support the belief while others dismiss it as mere superstition.

It is important to keep an open mind in order to understand these stories as rationally as possible, but where do we draw the line of skepticism? Is it about concrete evidence battling fanciful beliefs? Or is it more about accepting the data before proving it?

Researchers such as Dr. Jim B. Tucker and Dr. Ian Stevenson (both mentioned before) have documented several cases of people with vivid recollections of events, places, and people from a previous existence. These accounts, while anecdotal, have sparked interest among scientists who seek to understand the nature of consciousness and the possibility of memories transcending lifetimes.

Dr. Tucker has worked in the field for a couple of decades now, intent on getting closer to the truth with every new case he finds. As established in this *Journal of Scientific Exploration* paper, "Children Who Claim to Remember Previous Lives: Past, Present, and Future Research" (2007):

> Children's reports of past-life memories occur worldwide, and 2,500 cases have now been studied. Some of the children come from areas with a cultural belief in reincarnation, but some do not. In many cases, the child's statements have been verified to be accurate for one particular deceased individual. (Section "Explanations for the Cases")

Dr. Tucker goes on to explain how his findings include that children often have birthmarks or defects that reflect a mark or a wound from the bodies of their previous lives. Many of these children also show behavioral patterns consistent with events from their previous lives, especially when it comes to their deaths. When tested, they could explain and recognize people, situations, and places from their past lives, many of which have been verified by multiple reviewers.

Even if we call this a coincidence, it's a rather massive one and the odds of that are rather slim. At the very least, we must consider options beyond random occurrences if we are to keep this conversation alive.

Subjectivity for All

I find the notion of reincarnation intriguing and worthy of further exploration. The myriad cases explored around the planet offer incredibly distinct flavors to the melting pot of ideas about the afterlife.

In its quest to understand the mysteries of life, science has turned its gaze toward the concept of reincarnation. This ancient belief, which suggests that individuals can be reborn in new bodies after death, has captivated the human imagination for centuries. While science may not have all the answers, people have approached the topic with curious and clear minds, seeking to explore the possibility of past lives and the potential benefits of such knowledge.

Science is an excellent place to satiate curiosity using genuine data. When it comes to a field that boasts experiences and controversies galore, researchers dive deep to try and stay neutral and on course. The idea behind the research mustn't be to just prove the argument; it must be to find out the truth. If a researcher starts a study with the intent of only proving what they believe in, they may see only what they want to see. The ideal researcher accepts data for what it says without twisting it to suit their expectations.

Investigations have explored the potential therapeutic benefits of reincarnation beliefs. Some studies suggest that individuals who hold such beliefs may experience improved mental well-being and a greater sense of purpose in life. By embracing the idea that our current existence is just one chapter in a longer narrative, individuals may find solace and meaning in the face of life's challenges.

Studying past-life memories using PLR hypnosis is also an option. This is often taken with a grain of salt, but the underlying thought is that people's recollections are always subjective. I've mentioned this before. Subjectivity is difficult to transform into quantitative information to check and verify. Often impossible, as you will have learned from reading about the various memories of past lives as narrated by people, mostly children. Their unique perspective is the reason for the worn threads that build the fabric of this theory.

While science does not have definitive answers, the exploration of this topic demonstrates a willingness to explore the unknown. By examining past-life memories and considering the potential psychological benefits of believing in reincarnation, scientists, doctors, and professionals offer a fresh and trained perspective on the mysteries of life and death. Whether someone believes in the concept or not, it is clear that an objective but passionate approach is required to understand this human experience.

Reincarnation: A Source of Comfort and Understanding

I've always been drawn to the idea of reincarnation. It offers a tantalizing glimpse into the possibility of life beyond this realm.

As discussed, this concept is not without its fair share of skeptics. A significant portion of the population desires complete evidence and proven data before they choose to acknowledge this as a possibility. Rebirth offers a sense of hope and optimism, suggesting that our journey does not end with death. It presents the idea that we are part of a grand universal dance, constantly evolving and progressing toward a higher state of being.

Many of us have lost someone dear to us. We may know people who've had close brushes with death and who have changed so much in personality that we have nothing in common with them. When death comes so close, we're left reeling from the unbearable truth of the fragility of life.

Thinking about rebirth helps many people. We can Imagine that the ones we've lost are still out there making new friends and dancing to new tunes. We just aren't close to them anymore, but isn't it a comfort to know that they're still there?

For those who believe in samsara, reincarnation encourages personal responsibility and accountability. If we are to be reborn, then our actions in this life have consequences that extend far beyond our mortal existence. It reminds us to live with integrity, kindness, and compassion, knowing that our choices will shape not only our current lives but also our future ones.

This idea fascinates us in different ways. When we have a treasure trove like this, it's important not to dismiss it out of hand but to pay closer attention to how the idea makes us feel. It fills me with hope to imagine having multiple lives to get the full HD experience of this planet.

Imagine a single soul

- living in Cairo—indulging in a hundred varieties of food

- growing up in Mumbai—playing street cricket

- toddling about on the outskirts of Paris—ready for school in the big city

- studying in Tokyo—using the train as an independent child

- dancing in Rio de Janeiro—celebrating life with every colorful festival under the sun

- graduating in San Diego—ready to take on the world all over again!

It gives a whole other meaning to traveling around the world and experiencing a full lifetime's worth of beauty and brilliance. Such ideas often emphasize the interconnectedness of all living beings. They remind us that we are not alone in our struggles and triumphs, but that we are rather part of a vast web of souls that have traversed the realms of existence throughout history.

This realization fosters a sense of empathy and compassion as we come to understand that the joys and sorrows we experience are shared by countless others. It encourages us to treat others with kindness and understanding, recognizing that we are all on a journey of growth and self-discovery.

Reincarnation accounts have the power to enlighten and comfort us. They offer an out-of-the-box perspective on life and death, challenging our beliefs and expanding our understanding of the world. These recollections inspire us to reflect on our own existence and contemplate the possibility of multiple lifetimes. Whether we believe in reincarnation or not, these tales can teach us valuable lessons about compassion, empathy, and personal growth.

Chapter Seven

Soothing the Soul

Grieving, Healing, and the Afterlife

Death is nothing at all.
I have only slipped away to the next room.
I am I, and you are you.Whatever we were to each other,
That, we still are.

–Henry Scott Holland

When faced with loss, it's natural to search for answers to stall or soothe the turmoil. Many find that belief in an afterlife provides solace and comfort during the grieving process. It allows individuals to hold onto the hope of reuniting with their loved ones in another realm.

While grief may challenge our faith, it also deepens it by prompting a search for meaning and understanding. Reconciling grief with belief in the afterlife is a personal journey that varies for each person. Subjective interpretation and faith are vital for anyone looking out into the world to find hope in the matter of living a life without their loved one.

If there is a belief that offers comfort, even without evidence, rest assured people will spend time and energy finding out more about it. That's what love is all about.

The Many Faces of Grief

What Is the Soul?

Well, if you ever find a cohesive definition, let me know! All I can say is this: The soul is our consciousness filled with all our experiences, memories, and emotions. It's where our bodily instincts interact with our innate thoughts.

However, faiths may approach the question differently than science. Religions may talk of the soul as the essence of your life, a potent concoction of all your good and bad deeds to be judged before birth into the next life.

Conventional science emphasizes the value of every part of the body functioning simultaneously to keep life processes at optimal levels. The soul does not contribute to the body as every cell, nerve, and vessel does. Even so, we have a vague feeling of what's within us. Our drive to pursue passions and hobbies and our love for our friends and family are just a few of the ingredients that make each soul unique and a complete world in itself.

How Grief Affects Us: Body and Soul

A popular take on processing grief is Elisabeth Kübler-Ross's model of the five stages of grief. Denial, anger, bargaining, depression, and acceptance are certainly common phases in processing grief and pain, but I would say these stages aren't a strict sequence we'll all adhere to.

Some may combine denial and anger and rant about the unfairness of life while a few may even skip the stage of bargaining. Many may not even experience their grief in the same order, and others will have intense emotions of other kinds such as disgust and numbness. While not everyone will go through each stage, understanding these stages can be incredibly helpful in making sense of the emotional roller coaster that grief often is.

Do we struggle to accept the reality of our loss, or do we push ourselves to move on? Often, we find it difficult to accept that these things are out of our control. Our lives, families, friends, successes, careers, houses, and material possessions are simply not ours forever. And this is a hard lesson to accept. You'll come across people who choose to hold on for years, unable to simply let go because it's just not in their nature to do so.

This is represented in pop culture as well, with movies that discuss the mash of different faiths and how it affects people. For example, in the Marvel movie *Shang-Chi: The*

Legend of the Ten Rings, the Chinese-American characters talk about how a woman mourns her husband's passing by observing certain rituals that involve placing the deceased's favorite things by his grave. When the younger characters don't seem so taken by the idea, she feels they assume it's a silly notion.

The woman's granddaughter reassures her that, "We don't think it's silly, Waipo. We just know Waigong would've wanted you to move on and enjoy your life."

And the girl's mother chimes in, "Moving on is an American idea" (Cretton, 2021).

But more than an Eastern belief or Western dispute, many of us have an idea of what our souls are about. It's about the self and the choices we make for each other and ourselves. In this way, grief becomes the common enemy of the mind, body, and soul. All three aspects must bond and work together to get past this unfathomable depth of pain to help us reach peace.

People gradually come to terms with their pain in very different ways based on their beliefs, ideas, culture, and influences. Any state of extreme emotion is challenging, but it is an essential part of the healing process. Expecting a linear strategy of mourning is a decidedly bad plan. We can't simply direct our emotions. We must process them at a gentle pace. This requires seeking proper support, either from family or professional sources. By acknowledging and embracing these upheavals, we find healing and ultimately move toward acceptance.

Questioning Mortality

The loss of a loved one can cause profound existential breakdowns, leading to questions about mortality and the afterlife. It helps to remember that grief is always a personal journey that we are bound to navigate at some point in our lives.

Contemplating the afterlife is not only natural but also a sign of our deep desire for meaning and purpose in life. It's an intriguing subject that invites us to explore the unknown and challenge our understanding of the world around us. We wonder what happens to our loved ones when they're gone. Is there something beyond this earthly existence? Will we meet them again? Will we see them in the prime of their lives? Would they recognize us?

Posing these queries is innate and fundamental because they're our verbalized thoughts of pain, grief, and deep emotions.

It is a crisis of mortality that affects us. We ask the world why we deserve such a loss and are left shaken when answers never suffice. Nobody can explain death to an extent that will satisfy the world. Therefore, nobody is completely satisfied. We can find comfort in the choices we make, but it's jarring to remember that we can never control our fate and our mortality.

This is why many turn to discussions of the afterlife. If there is hope for life beyond death, it's comforting to know that we have not completely lost our loved ones. They're merely in another realm, one where we can rejoin them. The afterlife offers this solace we need in the face of mortality. It provides a sense of continuity and the hope of being reunited with loved ones who have passed away. The belief in an afterlife can bring comfort during times of grief and loss, offering the reassurance that death is not the end.

Questioning mortality leads to thoughts of potential reincarnation and peaceful afterlives rather than oblivion. As stated by Will Durant, "The hope of another life gives us courage to meet our own death, and to bear with the death of our loved ones; we are twice armed if we fight with faith" (1926, p. 35).

Grief and the Afterlife: A Link Belief Trumps Skepticism

Some say hope is a double-edged sword, quite as ready to hurt us as it is to protect us. Is it too wishful to imagine a world where nobody is lost and nobody loses? Must we grit our teeth and accept that the end is the end and that we may never see anyone again once we reach it?

No. I say no. I write no. I type no. I believe that there is something more out there for us.

I do not consider myself fanciful or fluttery or unaware of life's trials and tribulations. I have faced troubles, as have most people on this planet. I have seen the silver lining, something not enough of us have. I desire to bring you this strand of hope, to help you stay afloat with the life jacket till you reach a raft, a boat, a ship, or land.

This belief may not alleviate the pain and sadness associated with death, but it helps. It gives you the energy you need to keep moving through the molasses. Many find closure with the idea of a safe afterlife. People can find meaning in the new situation and can even translate the feelings of loss into something neutral or stronger.

For some of us, believing in the afterlife can be a source of strength and support for those experiencing loss.

The Lovely Afterlife

In taking the perspective that there is an afterlife and that it is wonderful, we can rest well knowing that people across the world are on our side. Let's take the case of near-death experiences again. We've explored many instances of NDEs in the previous chapters, but let's look at some more.

One of the more popular aspects of NDEs is that people encounter a world of heavenly bliss, perhaps communicating with their passed-on loved ones or higher divine beings of light.

It's fairly common in many experiences, as in the case of Dr. Melinda Greer who had a searing NDE when she was 55 and during it witnessed incredible love and compassion (Tamkins, 2023):

> As the nurse was performing CPR on her, Greer saw an "incredible white light" and felt "an incredible all-encompassing, all-surrounding sense of love." She felt like she had returned to a "place that felt like home to me, and I was back amongst a group of what I can only call beings, because we weren't physical, that I considered my group." (Section "All-Surrounding Sense of Love")

While a small portion of NDErs do experience hellish visuals, a significant portion talk about welcoming scenes of heavenly warmth and light. As Greer puts it, she seemed to have returned to the place of love rather than visiting it for the first time. It seemed to suggest that we are all from this place that we will go back to once our material lives come to a close.

Such an event is a stark reminder of our view of the world and life itself. It allows us to hold on to the belief that death is not the end but rather a transition to another realm. This belief often provides a feeling of well-needed closure and allows us to find meaning in the face of loss. While the afterlife may be a matter of faith rather than fact, it's a valuable tool for coping with grief and finding comfort in times of sorrow. But will you offer this option to people who struggle every day?

Long-Distance Connection

True strength is knowing that life is tough yet being compassionate despite hardships. Can you extend kindness to someone who is suffering, even if you're quite different from them in belief and culture? What's stopping you from doing so?

Perhaps there is more to it than simply "staying in your lane." And while we may not be able to physically connect with our loved ones, we can maintain a healing spiritual connection. But these beliefs remain personal and subjective. It can be a source of healing during times of grief. If it helps, it helps. I believe we can have a meaningful and healing spiritual connection with the departed.

This suggests that we're not alone even in death. Our experiences share a trademark identity with common events such as seeing the light, speaking with the deceased, and various out-of-body experiences. I believe this opens the possibility of continued connections beyond the physical realm. So, perhaps death is not the final goodbye. Rather it could be a transition into a different form of existence where relationships and connections can still be maintained. If people have sensed true love, compassion, and brilliance in their NDEs, then we can build on these concepts to say we can form connections with each other simply by believing in these links.

The key lies in embracing the journey and allowing ourselves to feel the depths of our emotions. It's through this process that we begin to heal and find a sense of peace. Once we're able to accept this ourselves, we can help others should they choose similar paths.

Coping Strategies: Healing Amid Loss
Self-Strategies

It's vital to take up mindfulness practices on a daily basis. This means being self-aware of your emotional well-being is just as important as looking out for your physical health. Everything adds up at the end of the day.

Oftentimes, you'll hear how deep meditation practices help people disconnect from the troubles of reality and sense the energies around them. These practices range in intensity and method based on the type of technique you follow. For example, transcendental meditation may work well for some folks while others benefit from a combination of meditation and deep breathing. But once you find your niche, you'll be able to de-stress and disconnect from the struggles of reality temporarily.

I don't mean magical energy; I mean metaphysical sensations that you feel when you're in a liminal space, open to connections. Properly done, meditation can relax the frantic energy in your body. This helps the mind dive into long-term memories to remember important events and therefore the emotions that went along with them. Successful sessions help people recall the presence of their loved ones and find comfort in this practice.

Helpful Rituals

It's not just about working on your inner fears. It's also about processing the grief. Avoiding pain is tantamount to postponing hurt to a different date.

You can take a cue from the practices of various faiths and cultures. In Mexico, *Día de los Muertos* is a day out of the year when people remember the deceased. The Day of the Dead is not just a mourning period but a beautiful commemoration of the memories of loved ones. People place photographs and artwork of their departed friends and family members on a pedestal called an *ofrenda*. They also place food and drinks by the grave sites in the belief that this is the one day when the deceased can visit the living.

There is no proof or scientific evidence. But this celebration needs none of those because Día de los Muertos is not just for the departed: It's for the people striving for prosperous lives without their loved ones.

The Torajan community in Indonesia performs elaborate funeral ceremonies for their deceased (McKay, 2019):

> When a loved one passes on, their families don't immediately prepare them for burial or cremation. Instead, the body is embalmed and kept in the family home and taken care of as if they were still alive. During this stage of the ceremony, Torajans don't even refer to their loved ones as dead but as makula, meaning one who is just sick. (Section "Living With the Dead")

The people spend days and wealth on this commemoration to ensure everyone is part of the grieving process. The focus is not on denying anything but rather on remembering the best aspects of life with this person and celebrating their exit from this world and their entrance to the next.

Similar death rituals across the world help people remember the good times and revel in their happiness rather than sink in the sadness. These ceremonies do not ignore the loss but rather help people process it as a community. Imagine thousands of people mourning someone only you knew personally. It's the ultimate proof that you aren't alone in this bereavement.

Support Systems

A family or a circle of trusted people must recognize the loss and what it entails for individual members of that circle. It's clear to everyone only when people are gently encouraged to share their experiences and pain. The loss essentially brings disorder to a previous status quo. People must realize that they need time to accept the loss and build a new normal to refocus duties, rewards, and breaks between everyone (Bacchus, 2021).

In other words, bereavement is a messy, nonlinear, and unscripted process. It's not just important to bring mourners back on track; the focus must be to address the pain. Normalcy has been displaced, and we must try and help each other while taking time off for our deepest anxieties to ebb away slowly.

Reach out to friend circles who are aware of your turmoil and who may have even experienced similar losses. They might offer help in ways you wouldn't have thought of. They can share techniques that helped them in their time of need. Or they can simply be an ear to listen and a shoulder to cry on.

Beyond families and friends, if you're part of religious or spiritual communities that share losses as much as successes, you'll find comfort in like-minded thinking. If you wish for a less faith-based strategy, find therapists and counselors who are professionally experienced to help you uncover the trauma and deal with it one day at a time. Similar online support groups and forums offer perspectives of shared experiences where you can put out your thoughts, emotions, and worries in safe spaces while receiving unconditional compassion and support.

It's important to find helpful groups that provide exactly what you need. Search for verified communities through people you know. Therapists who share your views on spirituality, religion, identity, race, and more are likely to help you in better ways than disparate people, but you never know. You may end up learning more than expected from people different from you.

Transforming Grief: Spiritual Growth From Loss

The world has experienced loss since its first birth millions of years ago. Elephants grieve their herd members for weeks. They have specific sites in their territory that are elephant graveyards for the ones who know their time has come. Dogs and cats often find secluded places away from communities to lie down and sleep until they pass away peacefully. Older wolves near death have been known to refuse to eat in order to save meat for the other members of the pack.

Have you ever imagined a herd of dinosaurs crying out in packs when they've lost a member? Do birds hesitate to take the spot of a deceased one during their regular flying formations? Is there a delay in ducklings imprinting on any animal, even humans, once their mother is gone?

Old literature may spout survival of the fittest, but the care and love between all living creatures must not be underestimated. I think about the pain and compassion between animals, not that's anthropomorphized but natural in its own way. Perhaps we can only understand them in human terms. Despite our different tongues, I believe we share languages of love and trauma across species and periods.

As mentioned before, people seek out various explanations for anything that offers them comfort in trying times. We're often not clear-sighted in our search in the immediate aftermath of devastating events, but we must not force ourselves to be. Clarity is within reach when we've had some time to process the pain. Once we gain that, we know how much of a reward it is to search for reasons rather than pinning an answer down.

We see this in the *Mind Body Green* article, "Following My Dad's Death, This Research Convinced Me of an Afterlife," where Elizabeth Entin explains how she tried to reconcile with her grief for her father who'd recently passed away by researching the afterlife (2021):

I find it very affirming to have science-mind-
ed research teams at major universities critically
studying the evidence of the afterlife and psychic
abilities ... Yes, I miss my dad every day, but it
brings me hope, joy, and fulfillment to think that
he is around me and that I will see him again. I
am someone who operates off of solid research
and evidence, not faith or belief. And I'm so glad
I've found it. (Section "The Bottom Line")

Entin's journey lands her with hopeful theories about the
afterlife, which include NDE possibilities and reincarnation.
They're never solid answers, but she acknowledges the solace
these beliefs have given her. Understanding that there may be
a chance she can meet her father again or even be assured that
he's in a genuinely good place now allows her to think about
his memories with fondness.

When we think back on the past, it is often in conjunc-
tion with the present's circumstances. Our past contains the
grooves of milestones that have solidified our personalities.
If you've ever found it difficult to learn new tricks or make
different choices, it's possible that the situation has a link to
something you've faced before.

Take NDEs, for example. People have life reviews or extended flashbacks to specific moments of their lives. They
may relive a distinct memory that formed a significant part

of their core personality, but this time, they see it from a third-person point of view. Perhaps these near-fatal experiences are a way to shine a light on the importance of the big and small moments. Rarely do people think about their material gains. Most NDEs and OBEs revolve around people, feelings, and the bonds formed all through life.

It's clear that confronting such a solid moment of mortality shifts perspectives. You're suddenly laser-focused on the truly important things in life. The ifs and buts fade into the background, and you may even wonder why such small worries ever slowed you down.

These are the truths that remind you of the true quality and strength of your soul. You desire to keep living and keep growing despite death looming over us all. As the musical *Hamilton* puts it so beautifully, "Death doesn't discriminate between the sinners and the saints. It takes and it takes, and it takes. And we keep living anyway" (Kail & Miranda, 2020).

Chapter Eight

Embracing the Rainbow

An Exploration of Diverse Afterlife Beliefs

*Religion is just a path for finding truth: Religion is not truth.
It is just a path. And different people follow different paths.*
—Anita Moorjani

Consider Planet Earth spoilt for choice. We have a lot of cultures and religions with their own ideas of what happens after death. Rather than fretting about which path to take, I'm thankful that generations of people before us have come so far in conceptualizing and updating their beliefs just for us to find one, or more, that really speaks to us.

I don't believe these religions compete with each other for the truth. They are interesting and intricate ingredients in a beautiful potpourri for the world. So, let's explore some of them to see how their approach to accepting the afterlife teaches us a thing or two.

The Cultural Mosaic: A Look at Global Beliefs on the Afterlife

Hope Reincarnate

Whether it's a faith, a culture, an ethnic belief, or an old tradition, we must include reincarnation in the world's literature tapestry. It's a sliding scale on how the afterlife is seen as a reward or punishment based on a person's actions in life.

In Buddhism, the soul is reborn into a new body after death. The reincarnation concept also thrives in Hinduism and Jainism, which are dominant in South-East Asia. To those who find this idea enticing and truly helpful to stave away the fear of death and cherish the value of life, Buddhism is invaluable. People who desire to be reassured of their base fears find peace in this concept.

Kami Travels

Every country has multiple cultures and faiths cohabiting the land mass. There is a Japanese system of rituals, Shintoism, which has lasted a long time and has even been influenced by Buddhism when the religion spread to the region (Danowski, n.d.).

In Shintoism, a person's body is inhabited by their kami, the spirit that is weak when it is in a body but strong when the person dies and can leave. The kami travels into the afterlife and looks over the living from there while Shinto believers offer prayers and rituals to the spirits. This equal exchange of respect and energy maintains the balance of life and death. The idea that we can help our deceased loved ones while their spirits watch over us is wonderful and soothing for anyone grieving.

The Eternal Dreaming

The Aborigines of Australia developed the concept of the Dreaming to explain an entire worldview of how the many things in nature function without human intervention. The idea underscores the explanation of how all living creatures and the universe were formed. The worldview provides the laws for living forms to follow, which include relationships, rituals, and various activities.

The afterlife ideal is about the ancestral spirits who set the laws. This is explained in this article by Working With Indigenous Australians (2020):

> It was the spirit ancestors who gave Aboriginal people the lores, customs, and codes of conduct, and who are the source of the songs, dances, designs, languages, and rituals that are the basis of

Aboriginal religious expression. These ancestors were spirits who appeared in a variety of forms. When their work was completed, the ancestral spirits went back into the earth, the sky, and into the animals, land formation, and rivers. The ancestor-beings are "alive" in the spirit of Australian Aboriginals. (Section "The Dreaming")

Such cultural beliefs play a significant role in shaping perceptions of the afterlife. The First Nation's concepts were popularized in academic streams and then pop culture, which allowed many interpretations (some wholesome, others caricatured) for people all over the world to absorb and understand.

Exploring the Western Perspective: A Glimpse Into Christianity, Cherokee, and Secular Views

Specific Concepts

From the ancient Greeks to modern Christians, we have a rich gathering of beliefs and stories built around multiple versions of the afterlife. Exploring these concepts in their context and their influence allows us to contemplate how people across time, culture, and regions reflected upon life and death and how their perspective shapes ours with every passing day. These Western ideas of the afterlife provide us all with a captivating peek into the mysteries of existence.

For example, to Catholics, Heaven is described as a place of eternal bliss for those who have lived a righteous life while hell is depicted as a place of eternal suffering for the wicked. Protestants focus on their belief in Jesus Christ and the teachings in the Bible, along with the concept that the deceased leaves the world and enters an afterlife. Neither focus on rebirth but rather a judgment of the soul.

The Cherokee Nation is another example of many who have a beautiful and diverse set of beliefs regarding the afterlife. After death, the deceased's spirit journeys to the Land of the Dead while avoiding or defeating the devil's tricks (Mika, 2022).

If the spirit is successful, they can rest in peace. If not, they must wander the living realm forever. The living families honor the spirits of their dead by ensuring they're buried in the earth to supply food for plants and animals. Many Native American traditions hold fast to the equal exchange of energy between humans and nature all through life and death.

Secular Perspective

A stronghold of secularism is that there is no divinity or afterlife. Thus, death marks the end of our existence, and there is no consciousness or continuation beyond the grave. While this is incredibly bleak to some, it's also an opportunity to fully appreciate the present moment. The fear of eternal damnation changes to the fear of complete nonexistence. Some people choose to embrace the fear instead of running from it. They gain strength from the idea that this life is the only one we have and the only time we have that truly matters.

But there's flexibility with secularism. People can choose to trust in an afterlife without accepting divine power. I believe it's up to the individual. Basically, with this idea, since we can't prove the presence or absence of an afterlife, it's really up to us.

The perception of the afterlife varies greatly across different global populations. Whether rooted in religious beliefs, cultural traditions, or secular ideas, these concepts give us meaning to what might otherwise be a straightforward understanding of life. While the specifics differ, the concept itself is a universal theme that speaks to our innate desire to escape oblivion and the hope of a greater existence beyond death.

Many feel they have more agency in this form since it allows for a wide range of beliefs, including reincarnation, judgment, oblivion, and an afterlife. Our imaginations and faiths decide what happens in the end. The Western perspective identifies the tentpole ideas of morality, choices, and actions when it comes to figuring out the afterlife.

Delving Into the Eastern Perspective: Buddhism, Hinduism, and Islam

Buddhists accept rebirth as a part of their beliefs. To them, samsara is the cycle of reincarnation to be broken from to attain liberation or moksha. People and their families embrace the idea when they see their proof of it in people. More than simply what the faith teaches, when people choose to accept the idea, it is a helpful and strengthening notion to be reminded of a higher power who adores and loves everyone.

Similar to Buddhism, Hinduism follows the afterlife belief of reincarnation, a cycle from which people must escape. Yet, in many of the cases studied by Dr. Ian Stevenson (mentioned before), the Hindu families who raised children who were allegedly reincarnated saw them as a blessing, a sign that the teachings of their faith were true and beautiful.

In Islam, the concepts of paradise and hell are central to the faith, with paradise being a place of eternal happiness and hell being a place of punishment. Their scriptures do not consider rebirth but rather judgment based on their deeds on Earth, signifying the power of choice for every person.

People of different cultures and countries contribute to the overall perspectives built up on the afterlife as a phenomenon. It's always helpful to delve into the historical and cultural context of these stories. By understanding the time period and societal beliefs in which such tales originated, we have a better grasp of their significance.

Navigating Doubts: Addressing Common Questions About Diverse Afterlife Beliefs

It's quite a challenge to bring about harmony between people with various afterlife beliefs. A person can believe in an idea with all their heart, and it's a real shock to cross paths with a soul who has a worldview that knocks them off their feet.

Open-mindedness is always critical in these conversations. People who have grown up in very different parts of the world understand from a diverse point of view compared to others. It's hard to find a common ground. Often you won't be able to compromise, but this shouldn't lead to arguments and blows.

You can perhaps focus on the shared values of these different belief systems. Most religions emphasize the need to be kind to thy neighbor. This involves respecting their views as long as nobody's life and dignity are impeded. In the end, everyone is entitled to their faith since they derive solace and strength from their chosen belief systems. We must not begrudge those in search of answers and revelation just because they choose a different path.

Some people are raised in a particular faith but find comfort and understanding in the beliefs of another system. Others prefer to let go of all faiths in order to choose specific ideas from different systems. A few may be atheistic, preferring purely scientific views of the afterlife.

For example, people from various countries may adore the Buddhist idea of death as a transition into another life rather than an end. In the same vein, the secular concept of energy transformation (where matter is neither created nor destroyed, simply transformed all the time) offers visible ideas to people who desire proven evidence. We may not understand their journey, but that must not stop us from having strong bonds with them.

Embracing the Mystery: Finding Comfort in Diverse Beliefs

Here's your daily reminder that there is no definitive answer to what happens after we die. The different religions and cultures saturating the world with possibilities and hope are all we have.

We have a fair idea of what many spiritual and religious systems offer us. You can even read religious texts in recommended translations, attend well-conducted services and ceremonies, and engage in discussions with people of various faiths to gain a broader perspective. The more ideas we learn and question, the closer our approach to the truth.

A recent survey was done on people who've had out-of-body experiences and gone on to significantly transform their lives. It demonstrated how people who were generally religious (regardless of background) felt affirmed in their beliefs after experiencing OBEs. They acknowledged the presence of a divine deity and felt a beautiful connection to the universe on a grand level (Shaw et al., 2023). It shows how people's interpretation of their experiences sent them in the direction of believing or imagining that there is more to the cosmos than what is apparent.

You can make this discussion multilayered by involving philosophical ideologies of the afterlife. The ancient Greek philosophers Socrates, Plato, and Aristotle had their unique takes on death and the afterlife that have been infused in their teachings for millennia. More modern thinkers such as Descartes and Kant had discussed similar metaphysical topics of existentialism.

I find this passage from the book, *Evidence of the Afterlife*, incredibly engaging when we talk of religion and spiritual connections (Long & Perry, 2010):

> This book has important implications for religion. The great religions have always spoken to the belief in God and an afterlife ... Near-death experiences consistently reveal that death is not an end but rather a transition to an afterlife. This

is a profoundly inspiring thought for us all and
for our loved ones. (Section "Conclusion")

Exploring these theories from a theological or scientific
perspective provides new ideas of life, death, and the afterlife.
And by accepting and even cherishing that we may never fully
comprehend them, we can be satisfied with the vastness of
possibilities and the wonder of the human spirit.

Chapter Nine

Love and Compassion

The Soul's Language

Why choose to be good every day if there is no guaranteed reward we can count on, now or in the afterlife? I argue that we choose to be good because of our bonds with other people and our innate desire to treat them with dignity. Simply put, we are not in this alone. –Michael Schur, Kate Gersten, & Cord Jefferson

H ave you heard the line "life's not fair" at least once? Or a few times, or a lot? I bet you the people who said it were quoting a book or something, or they'd had their fair share of troubles and found it difficult to look on the bright side of things.

What if I told you life, as a general concept of probabilities and natural events, rarely discriminates, and it's people who show judgment and prejudices? You probably knew that. But it doesn't hurt to have the reminder.

It's not easy to be happy, caring, and compassionate 24/7. The real effort put into being kind to others must not be overlooked by any measure. It's difficult to show kindness to yourself on some days. Nobody said we have to be perfectly open, candid, and good all the time. It's not possible to do so.

So, use those times as a reset for your soul. Assess your energy, figure out where you are in life, and understand that your perspective is incredibly subjective.

This is where we bring back the absolute overhaul of near-death experiences. As we've discussed, NDEs elicit a system reset of your view of the world. Suddenly, material goals may seem lacking. You may have altered passions and ideas to pursue or express different attitudes to old things by embracing or rejecting them. Let's take a look at the range of possibilities an NDE provides.

The Power of Love: Recurring Themes in Near-Death Experiences

Universality

NDEs have been known to shower the experiencer with grand and overwhelming love. This alone is enough to permanently change people because, in today's age, we're not really used to complete and unconditional love in a permanent sense. We face problems and hardships that remind us how fragile our luck can be. Any instance of misfortune may be called karma, and a fortunate occurrence could be kismet. We have no rationale for so many things that happen in our lives every day.

This is why NDEs have the remarkable ability to evoke a sense of love for people. It's as if these encounters with the afterlife unlock a deep well of compassion within us, reminding us of the importance of human connection. The experience often leaves people with a profound appreciation for the beauty and complexity of human relationships, leading to a greater desire to nurture and cherish those around them.

In the groundbreaking publication, *Beyond the Light*, Robin Halberdier recounts her NDE as an infant struggling with Hyaline membrane disease. Her first memory is that of bright light. When she survived the episode and made it to toddler age and began speaking, she told her parents of the experience of light (Atwater, 1994):

> There was a standing figure in the light, shaped like a normal human being, but with no distinct facial features. It had a masculine presence. The light I have described seemed like it emanated from that figure. Light rays shone all around him. I felt very protected and safe and loved. "The

figure in the light told me through what I now
know to be mental telepathy that I must go
back, that it was not time for me to come here.
I wanted to stay because I felt so full of joy and
so peaceful." (p. 13)

Robin went on to describe a glass case that she vaguely
recalled which actually turned out to be the incubator
from when she'd been admitted to hospital as a newborn.
Her father was a medical student at the time of this telling
and had read up on NDEs, immediately connecting her
experience to one.

It seems astounding that an infant could recall a scene of
pure light and brilliance from such a young age. But perhaps that's to be expected. This form of love may surpass
any form of negativity and connect all earthly beings at a
fundamental level, that level being that we deserve to be
dignified and loved.

Personal Transformation

The impact of NDEs on people is undeniable. We've read
narratives of many who have gone through these experiences and reported a newfound sense of empathy and understanding toward others. The love they felt during their
encounter with the afterlife stays with them, transforming
their outlook on life and relationships.

This newfound love extends beyond family and friends, encompassing a deep compassion for all of humanity. It's a warmth that transcends boundaries and unites us as a species. I don't believe this is a mere coincidence. There must be a connection between the experiences of people from Japan and the US, for example. When so many people describe being enveloped in a profound sense of love and acceptance, we know there's more to this than meets the eye. This idea alone infuses an NDEr with a brighter and stronger outlook on life. They've experienced a love that was unlike anything experienced in the physical world, regardless of faith, culture, and identity—a benevolence that is all-encompassing, unconditional, and often beyond words.

Dr. Margot Grey has researched accounts of people who have been close to death or survived a clinical death. She recounts them experiencing attitude changes and a more developed perspective on life (Taylor, 2018):

> People often report becoming more intuitive, too. [A] woman told Margot Grey that she felt "a very heightened sense of love, the ability to communicate love, the ability to find joy and pleasure in the most insignificant things about me ... I seemed to have a very heightened awareness, I would say almost telepathic abilities." (Section "The After-Effects of NDEs")

When a harrowing experience can bring inexplicable peace and potential joy, it's worth researching. As seen, this overwhelming feeling of love can have a transformative effect on individuals, leading them to re-evaluate their priorities and make positive changes in their lives.

Cross Connections

In fact, after witnessing the secrets of the cosmos and how the universe is in motion around us all, returning to mundane life may feel like a step back for some. But the realization seeps in when someone is able to put into effect what they learned from their NDE. For example, bigotry against base differences seems immaterial when we consider the grand scale of everything there has ever been.

In an episode of Jay Shetty's podcast where he interviews Tom Holland, the actor speaks of a time he and his friends vacationed in Mexico. They had been diving when they came face to face with an immense whale. Holland states that he looked right at the creature and was aware of how hauntingly peaceful the moment was (2023):

> I think part of the reason why I felt so calm when the whale had come up was because there was nothing we could do should it go sideways. Yeah, and I think of almost finding that kind of inner peace of, like, I've made my mind this is the

choices I've made I'm here now there's nothing
I can do. It's almost like you should make peace
with your choices. (1:32:09)

When we stand in front of Death's door, knowing that it can swing open at any time, knowing that a gust of wind is all that it takes to make us stumble through it, we are the most aware we'll ever be. Self-awareness and mindfulness of the world around us are practically superpowers when you consider how people can be incredibly closeted by their deadlines, goals, worries, and wins.

This mindfulness can be considered a byproduct of recognizing the connection between people of various countries, between individuals of different species, and indeed, between any soul you come across on a day-to-day basis. Such experiences serve as a powerful expression of the capacity for love within each of us. When we go out of our way to find the connections rather than the disparities, we're one step closer to the truth.

Compassion: The Bridge to Understanding Others

Change Your World

Extraordinary encounters with the afterlife change people; there's no doubt about that. In the best of situations, people attain a strong moral compass ruled by compassion. It feels deserved after they've glanced at a realm where empathy reigns supreme.

Returning from the brink of death and witnessing the afterlife are perhaps the greatest struggles for the living. Is it really a surprise to watch people take this second shot at life with a renewed sense of purpose, with a compassionate personality? The capacity for such love has always been in every one of us. NDEs seem to be a catalyst for many to show explicit sympathy and care for the world.

Beyond their immediate lives, stories of NDE survivors have been known to motivate others as well. Can one person inspire a collective? Can one experience change a community? Absolutely! It lets us know that compassion is not an optional virtue but a fundamental quality of humanity.

Inexplicable Chance

Excellent nurturing is often the source of compassion and love for others. In other cases, people are faced with brutally honest information about themselves which encourages them to make proper changes. NDEs are capable of this, but there have been instances where people wake up from near-fatal situations and have unexplained changes in their personalities.

In 2004, Salimah had a life-saving surgery to remove a large tumor from her temporal lobe. Following the event, she had a distinct personality shift with no explanation as to why. As a chemist, she had always been excellent at her job, but now she was welcoming and more social toward others. As seen in an article in *The New Yorker* by Oliver Sacks (2007):

> Salimah's new cheerfulness was apparent at work. She had worked in the same laboratory for fifteen years and had always been admired for her intelligence and dedication. Yet, while losing none of this professional competence, she seemed a much warmer person, keenly sympathetic and interested in the lives and feelings of her co-workers. Where before, in a colleague's words, she had been "much more into herself,"

she now became the confidante and social center
of the entire lab. (para. 20)

Doctors will explain these changes by focusing on neuroscience and how the brain and its cells have been altered by the
life-changing event. I certainly believe this is a partial truth.
There is always the chance that people unconsciously change
to be better versions because, in a utopia, those are the kind
of people we'll always find.

Healing Spark

Dr. Jeffrey Long and Paul Perry's work with NDE survivors
is documented in their book *Evidence of the Afterlife*. It contains upward of 600 accounts of NDEs, several of which have
afterlife scenes that talk of the place of love infusing their
souls with the same compassion and brightness. The authors
observe (Long & Perry, 2010).

> For me personally, I'm showing more love
> to others now than before I started my
> near-death-experience studies. My understand-
> ing of near-death experiences has made me a bet-
> ter doctor. I face life with more courage and con-
> fidence. I believe NDErs really do bring back a
> piece of the afterlife. When NDErs share their
> remarkable experiences, I believe a piece of the

afterlife, in some mysterious way, becomes available to us all. (Section "Conclusion")

Some of the more consistent reports by NDE survivors have included seeing life reviews, witnessing beings of light and love, and glimpsing heavenly (or even hellish) afterlives. To be in the presence of NDErs is to admit that we sense the change in them and the kind of person they wish to be now.

Sympathy and compassion encourage more than an improved personality. Communities can become motivated spheres of living where people interact and gain help through avenues that dismiss tough love or negative reinforcement scenarios.

An example is compassion-focused therapy (CFT), which is a fairly new approach to therapy sessions. Conceptualized by Paul Gilbert in the early 21st century, he proposed CFT as an overall approach for integrated psychological treatments. The effectiveness will be apparent, as stated here (Leaviss & Uttley, 2014):

> Individuals with a highly self-critical "inner voice" may struggle with other evidence-based therapies, so helping these individuals to develop a more compassionate, encouraging "inner voice" may enable better engagement. CFT is therefore proposed for use as a multi-modal therapy, based

on a scientist–practitioner model rather than belonging to a single "school of therapy." (Section "Core Principles of CFT")

CFT has been useful in treating cases of mental health issues. The therapeutic potential seems to go without saying, but with a science-backed explanation of why compassion truly helps, people gain a better quality of help.

If this is a lesson in compassion, it's a well-taught one. The key takeaway is to strive to be more compassionate toward others, for it is through acts of kindness that we make a difference in people and the world.

Compassion Toward Others

When faced with the unconditional love and acceptance that is often reported in NDEs, individuals may feel a deep sense of connection to others and a desire to treat others with kindness and understanding. This can lead to a shift in perspective, with individuals placing greater importance on love, compassion, and personal growth.

We're not alone in this journey of sharing time and space. If you have not heard of Anaheim School District's Million Acts of Kindness story, you're in for a treat! This is one of the many beautiful examples of the incredible power of kindness.

In 2013, Tom Tait (then mayor of Anaheim, California,) started the Year of Kindness Campaign. He asked the students to come up with random acts of kindness that were simple yet wonderful. And they did it! The school district completed a cool million acts of kindness that improved the community as a whole (Dienstman, 2019):

> Not only do these random acts of kindness make someone's day, but they have a proven positive impact on society. The city and school district report lower detention rates along with a decrease in aggressive behavior. Tait's kindness movement has become an aspiration for today's society. Going beyond elementary students, applying these kind gestures to our everyday lives can make the world a better place. (para. 9)

Their kindness wasn't flashy. It involved simple acts such as opening the door for others and greeting and cheering each other up. The long-term effects managed to reduce acts of bullying and violence during this period.

Such acts are possible all around the world, motivating people to come together and do amazing things for their less fortunate neighbors. This kind of inspiration and love can come from anyone—your friend, family, coworker, and indeed, from your own experiences, subtle and otherwise.

The revelation of the power of love experienced during NDEs can encourage personal transformation to do exactly what I've outlined above. The powerful sense of compassion reported by NDE survivors can and has inspired people to live stronger and truer lives, prioritize love and compassion, and make positive changes. It seems like a glimpse into the heavenly afterlife affords us all a glimpse into the best versions of ourselves.

Overcoming Barriers to Love and Compassion

Change for the Better

In a world where we often feel disconnected and divided, the power of love and divinity experienced during NDEs offers us hope. It serves as a reminder that love is a powerful force that can bridge gaps and heal wounds.

This positivity encourages us to prioritize kindness and compassion in our interactions with others. We know that these small acts of love can have a ripple effect, spreading positivity and unity throughout various communities. NDEs remind us of the incredible potential for love that exists within each of us, and they inspire us to embrace it fully in our lives. Reminders of powerful compassion can truly change us for the better.

Dr. Tony Cicoria was an orthopedic surgeon in 1994 when he was struck by lightning and experienced an unearthly NDE. Granted, no NDE is earthly, but Cicoria shared how he'd been on his way up to a paradisical place before a good Samaritan administering CPR brought him back.

He recovered from his injuries in a few months and was even cleared to perform surgeries again, but Cicoria was taken over by a passion for music. He'd learned the piano as a boy but had not touched one for nearly three decades. Following this urge, he bought sheet music and taught himself how to play (Sacks, 2007):

> In the third month after being struck by lightning, then, Cicoria—once an easygoing, genial family man, almost indifferent to music—was inspired, even possessed, by music, and scarcely had time for anything else. It began to dawn on him that perhaps he had been "saved" for a special purpose. "I came to think that the only reason I had been allowed to survive was the music," he said. (para. 13)

Cicoria continued his practice as a surgeon while diving deeper into the insatiable need to compose complex piano rhythms. He had music in his head, convinced the songs were symphonies from heaven. It transformed his view of the world, and he divided his time between music, career, and life.

NDE transformations seem like the ultimate deus ex machina in real life. Surviving one nearly guarantees a complete turnaround, where the barriers of vulnerability, rejection, past hurt, and unawareness of others' struggles—especially with societal prejudices of race, gender, sexuality, and ethnicity—are broken.

Cultivate Support

Genuine sympathy helps people align tasks that promote compassion, inclusivity, and community. Let's start with a few tips to get a cycle of kindness going!

- **Communication:** Effective communication requires listening well. In order to get our points across, we must be willing to listen to other parties when they speak up. Only by ensuring communication flows well in all directions, will everyone's voices be heard and everyone's perspectives be utilized.

- **Patience:** Some people may take a while to formulate their thoughts to make solid decisions. They may be anxious about having the spotlight on them, and this can lead to inner turmoil that is exacerbated by people who egg them on and annoy them. It always helps to talk it out and give them just a bit more time to get things in perspective.

- **Respect:** To have a strong sense of camaraderie, we must respect each other's boundaries and ideas before starting arguments against them. We can disagree with each other's opinions, but there's a line we must not cross to avoid disrespecting each other's identity and dignity.

Don't wait for a life-threatening moment to be a better person. Oftentimes, the only person blocking your way to a kinder version of yourself is society's traditional expectations. It takes true bravery to dismantle them, so seek a trusted group to help you be compassionate to yourself and others.

Chapter Ten

The Practical Path

Integrating Spiritual Insights Into Everyday Life

There is no night without a dawning
No winter without a spring
And beyond the dark horizon.
Our hearts will once more sing
–Helen Steiner Rice

It remains difficult to recognize the finality of death in this life and to accept that time separates us all. When faced with loss, we need the time to truly process that. We cannot be calm, cool, and collected through all the events of our lives. No living being functions in that way.

So how do we use our comprehension skills to apply spiritual knowledge to daily life? How do we interpret such knowledge well enough in the first place? The last chapter of this book will focus on the ideas that come with this understanding. Remember that spirituality is not necessarily about religious sentiments, but it is an all-inclusive concept that the universe plays a vital role in our choices and our lives.

I believe this is what the afterlife visuals of NDEs have the potential to inspire in all of us. A brief glimpse of beauty and happiness can provide hope to those of us hitting rock bottom. We are all deserving of it.

The Power of Introspection: Reflecting on Spiritual Insights

Introspection has many use cases, especially when we consider the field of inquiry. On an everyday basis, it means considering a self-analysis of our actions, decisions, and results in order to make better choices in the future.

In the field of psychology, introspection is closely connected to exploring your mental and emotional state of health. It's a slightly more formalized concept than self-introspection, but the result is similar.

When done properly, introspection is an excellent tool to enhance growth and change for the better. For example, when a person embraces the pain that comes with thinking back on a near-death experience, they may come away feeling exposed to the raw emotions of the event. It's not pleasant or particularly desired, but the consequence is that the person can learn more about themselves and how their mind and body work in such dangerous situations.

More than that, they're able to recall how they responded to afterlife imagery from the event. An adrenaline rush is nothing to scoff at. High-pressure situations often reveal a person's resilience. You find out exactly what you're capable of in times of stress. Not many people like such situations, but it can take a trial by fire to discover your strength.

Self-reflection is an excellent aspect of introspective journeys. Reflecting on our feelings and thoughts helps us examine our past choices from a removed perspective. When we're not so attached to the moment, we have a clearer idea of what happened and how we could have altered it by approaching the decision from another angle. Instead of wishing we could have made a better choice, we'll learn how to approach a similar situation in a smarter and stronger way.

Proper reflection improves our ability to be more self-aware. This is the type of insight into your abilities and setbacks that benefits you in the long run. Sometimes, there are small parts of your personality that you may be encouraged to change. These simple changes can lead to better results and surprising outcomes. For example, you can learn to hold back loud reactions to unfavorable reviews of your work. This also improves your resilience to bad news and terrible situations. You can learn to vent in more productive ways, thereby making sure to not hold onto the negativity for long periods.

Not all NDEs are capable of this. It's more reflective of the person making decisions than the experience itself. Are you able to take a horrifying event and transform it into great potential? It's alright if you need help to do so. That's what sources of help like this book and your friends are for!

Try journal writing. Diary entries and journal prompts are excellent ways to start your introspective journey. At the end of the day, think back on the moments that stand out in your memories and write about how you felt about your actions or those of others. Sometimes, you may have a different thought process in the evening as compared to the morning.

The entries need not be just about your work. You can write about your chores, small tasks, and children as well. Try out some of these prompts:

- Reflect on a moment today that made you feel proud of yourself.

- Write about a moment today that made you feel you could have made a better decision.

- Reflect on the biggest change in yourself thanks to what you saw in your NDE or OBE.

Applying Spiritual Insights: Practical Steps

NDEs prove to be the most extraordinary encounters with the afterlife and also provide people with a strong appreciation for life. NDErs have experienced profound peace and love from their unfathomable experiences. I've brought up how transformative these moments are for people, and I'll say it again: NDE survivors have witnessed the other side of the equation and come back to tell how precious this life is!

Simply believing in the idea of the afterlife can show behavioral change. For instance, an American Psychological Association study focused on people with religious and afterlife beliefs and made a connection to their level of planetary sustainability. It showed how some U.S. citizens following Eastern traditions of Buddhism, Sikhism, and more understood the belief of reincarnation to be their directive. Thus, they put in more effort to support Earth's sustainability since they would be reborn on this planet again (Johnson et al., 2023).

Everyone searches for something that gives them meaning in their lives. For some, it's the understanding of why we're here at all. Do we live in this life to ensure the next one is worthwhile? Or does everything important happen here, in this moment in time?

If you need some helpful conversations, find a trusted family member or friend you can rely on. Check with them if they can act as a sounding board for you. Describe your worries and decisions and see how they respond.

It's up to you to see if their reactions are what you need or if you ought to change your approach. You can attempt this with a therapist as well to gain a professional perspective and advice to help you.

NDEs have encouraged people to live as their authentic selves and not put on a show for others. Your true self is what shines the brightest and inspires others. So, embrace these lessons and know that you stand to gain so much more from a fulfilling and purpose-driven life.

Transformative Stories: Learning From Others' Journeys

Stories of people changing their lives after terrible events are available all over the Internet. Brushes with death are the fastest and most horrific ways to bring forth the value of life in the clearest style.

Howard Storm was a chairman of the Northern Kentucky University's art department. Following a serious NDE during a trip to Paris, he re-evaluated his life and changed tracks. His religious devotion was at its peak, and Storm completed his Masters at the United Theological Seminary and was ordained. He served as the pastor of two Ohio churches while writing and painting on the side. He finds this gentler pursuit of happiness much more his speed than the ambitious track at the university.

Dr. Bruce Greyson explained this desire to change careers in an interview with *Newsweek* (Georgiou, 2021):

> I've seen career military people or policemen who could not tolerate the idea of hurting someone after their near-death experience change careers. I've seen cut-throat businessman who decided that competition was silly after a near-death experience change careers. And they typically go into helping professions—medical care, teaching, social work, or clergy, something like that. (para. 7)

Many switch from successful paths to happier ones. Some may even go the other way. It's less about what the world assumes and more about what the individual desires to do. Often, we tend to find ourselves swerving toward what others want us to do so we can gain their appreciation. But this does not fulfill our wants in the long run.

For a few people, it takes a drastic event to give them the bravery to live life on their terms. As much as we applaud them, we must be kind to them for this courage, just as we must show compassion to those who change their lives without an NDE or any form of disastrous moment. Some can be motivated by these stories alone, and this is why we must uphold all those who want their voices to be heard.

Cultivating an Open-Minded Approach: Exploring Diverse Perspectives

Multiple Theories Cohabit Peacefully

Every theory of the afterlife presents a unique interpretation of what can happen beyond death. It's not just the search for truth—it's all about humanity's curiosity and hope boiled down to an imaginative exploration of what could be. The variety of ideas offers us intellectual stimulation as well. When the world is open-minded, our possibilities grow endless.

A person in one corner of the world may imagine a possibility that helps not just them but thousands and millions of people across the planet. If one idea offers such wide-ranging comfort to those grappling with their mortality, a dozen ideas need not bring friction but rather hope for so many more. This is the beauty of diversity, especially since no afterlife theory is a one-size-fits-all answer.

Debating these ideas is the frontier to dispelling fear of the unknown. No matter your religion, belief, culture, and overall identity, you will have wondered about your end-of-life situation and what happens after death. When you have several helpful ideas trying to transform your gut fear into tentative hope, it's time to appreciate the vastness of human thought.

It helps to encourage and acknowledge this diversity. We are not forced to believe in all of these beliefs. We can pick and choose what helps us, just as we must allow others to choose what aids them. Nobody's choice must impinge on another's. This is how we accept and foster an inclusive society where people are free to explore their spiritual journeys without prejudice.

When people recognize the positivity of all these theories coexisting on a single plane, hope meets practicality. Everyone lives complex and real lives with struggles and squabbles. Often, we're simply not aware of our neighbors' problems and why they believe in certain things that seem outlandish to us. But it is what it is, and we can acknowledge things that help others, even if those ideas don't help us.

Reading Resources

Try out some extended reading that explores the afterlife from various standpoints. It always helps to know more as you decide what works for you and how it can help you come to terms with the delicate balance between life and death.

- Bruce Greyson, M.D., has a book titled *After: A Doctor Explores What Near-Death Experiences Reveal About Life and Beyond*. He writes about alternate theories and how his decades' worth of studies in

NDEs and the afterlife have opened a world of new perspectives to him.Resource Link 1: www.goodre ads.com/book/show/53137911-after

- Anita Moorjani's popular work, *Dying to Be Me: My Journey From Cancer, to Near Death, to True Healing*, recounts her personal tale of how she experienced a powerful NDE and later transformed her life.Resource Link 2: www.goodreads.com/book/s how/12291050-dying-to-be-me

- William Hasker's entry in the Stanford Encyclopedia of Philosophy is titled "Afterlife." He breaks down the material aspects of what the afterlife can mean in connection to parapsychology and NDEs. Hasker also offers further reading material in his article.Resource Link 3: plato.stanford.edu/entrie s/afterlife

- Steve Stewart-Williams's essay in *The Oxford Handbook of the Psychology of Religion* is titled "Afterlife Beliefs: An Evolutionary Perspective." He shows a philosophical and religious connection to the construction of afterlife beliefs, explaining why we as a species have developed these theories.Resource Link 4: www.researchgate.net/publication/324673914 Afterlife_beliefs_An_evolutionary_approach

At the end of the day, the beauty of many afterlife theories keeps us hoping for the best. Humanity's ability to inspire curiosity, provide comfort, and promote tolerance is the best result of the entire concept.

Navigating Life's Challenges: The Role of Spiritual Insights

Overpowering encounters with the afterlife often provide people with the curiosity to know more about their purpose and existence. I've mentioned before how NDEs seem to imply an interconnectivity between all living creatures on a cosmic level.

Recognizing this unity helps empower and encourage people to reach out to the community and socialize. It's a rediscovery of the love and kindness that are keys to our lives. NDE survivors have spoken at length of the love they've felt in their experience of the afterlife. This is the common denominator that brings us all together: the shared wanting of unconditional love that goes beyond what we may fathom.

We've talked about how such revelations push people to make vital changes in their lives, move careers, open discussions of deep and strong emotions with their families, and even reach out to people who have been out of the picture for a long time. This sudden understanding of the importance of meaningful living is not unheard of. In fact, prioritizing personal growth and relationships over material wealth is often the case with many NDErs. The altered perspective removes our rose-tinted glasses or overt negativity to help re-evaluate our lives in order to pursue what we truly exist for.

This is a lesson that can work for anyone who has not even had an NDE. People love the concept of changing their goals with absolutely no guilt over who they may disappoint. Even better is when we're encouraged to go after this happiness by our support systems.

Take, for example, movies and shows that motivate people to try new things. A fan-favorite movie of 2022 is *Puss in Boots: The Last Wish*, which shows how the protagonist comes across the character of Death through his journey. The story depicts how we can find ourselves amid the noise of fame and fortune. Puss, who has squandered his eight lives without really valuing them, is now forced to confront the fact that he has just one life left to live.

Family therapists Jonathan Decker and Emma McAdam discuss with Alan Seawright (the filmmaker) the significance of Puss choosing to fight for his last life (Cinema Therapy, 2023):

> I think like Puss in Boots, we are all aware that we're going to die one day, but we don't like to dwell on it, and it doesn't feel real. And so we kind of live our lives as if we're not going to. And

we live our lives wrapped up in the stupid daily crap, and the petty things that we get hung up on, or the pursuits that are kind of meaningless. Because if we actually make peace with "I'm going to die," then we would spend our time better. (22:44)

That's the first and best lesson of life and death. Remember that life is precious. Sometimes, NDEs provide a turning point in people's lives by demonstrating brilliance in adversity. Whether we have one life or nine, we can make sure the current one is as meaningful as possible.

Conclusion

Seeing death as the end of life is like seeing the horizon as the end of the ocean. –David Searls

D eath is a certainty. The beyond is a mystery. Decoding this has always been about the discussions with each other rather than hitting upon a solitary answer. Some are lucky to escape with a grand appreciation of this transient life. Some are lucky to pass, feeling no fear or worry.

Believing in an afterlife is a powerful tool for managing and thriving in life. It provides us with a sense of purpose and comfort by knowing that there is something beyond our earthly existence. It's a form of acceptance that helps us navigate the challenges of life, giving us a sense of hope and resilience. Our belief in something (anything!) allows us to find meaning in our experiences and make sense of the world around us. Really, embracing the idea of an afterlife offers many of us the strength and motivation we've been looking for for a long time.

Acceptance Through Variety

Here's a crash course on tolerance and acceptance!

Tolerance is about acknowledging diversity and understanding that different people find solace and build identities in various ways. Even if we don't necessarily agree with others, we need not stop them from continuing as they are. This means recognizing that we don't have all the answers and that there is value in hearing different viewpoints. By practicing tolerance, we create an environment where everyone can go about their lives without feeling the need to hide the less popular notions about their background or opinions. It opens the space for potential conversations that can lead people out into a more benevolent territory.

Acceptance is the gold mine. It's about truly respecting and embracing people for who they are, without unfair judgment. When we make the effort to appreciate the uniqueness of every individual, each with their own strengths and weaknesses, we create a different and more constructive space where people feel safe to be their authentic selves. This builds a sense of belonging and allows for healthier personal growth and self-acceptance.

By leaping off of this, you'll understand that acceptance is much more open and stronger than tolerance. But consider them as stepping stones. A person may begin at an egocentric level where their opinions are perfect and everyone else is wrong. By acknowledging the world and its mysteries, people can move up the levels, slowly learning more and understanding how to tolerate different perspectives. The more they grasp, the better they do this. When they're able to reach the level of acceptance and love, people are ready to embrace the world for the very diversity that they may have shunned before.

Sure, not everyone follows this route, but many of us are on this path. When someone else's experiences cannot be proved by science, must we jump to the conclusion that they are therefore untrue? We simply have not found ways to acquire solid data on such matters. I recall the age-old comparison to Thomas Edison's struggles with inventing the light bulb. He attempted and failed nearly 2,000 times to build the perfect circuit arrangement. That certainly made others say that electricity could not produce light in such a small instrument. However, once Edison found success and let his light bulb speak for itself, there were no naysayers.

If it's a matter of time, can we afford it? I think so. As a global village, we must listen to each other and understand that things that seem so far out need not necessarily be out of hand. So, once we accept an idea of life's (and death's) mystery, can we accept more simultaneously?

It's not just judgment or rebirth that we need to consider. People may mix and match their hopes for the beyond. Without proof, it's all down to our beliefs and intentions. Do we intend to soothe our worries or to pester others into adopting our ideas? That's important, and it's alright to take a step back to reconsider your approach at any point in your life.

For example, the concept of reincarnation may not be everyone's cup of tea, but I find it to be a fascinating and empowering belief. It offers a fresh perspective on life and death, inviting us to explore the idea that our souls are eternal and ever evolving. So, why not embrace the possibility of multiple lives? After all, it adds depth and meaning to our existence and encourages us to live with purpose and intention.

This works for me. It may not align with your self-interests, and that's alright! Similarly, your beliefs are perfect for you and may not suit others. True, part of unconditional love is affording the choice for all. It's about creating a space that's safe and where you can be brave to make your decisions and declare them without retaliation. I offer this to you. My book is your safe space. Choose to do what you will with this.

The Two-Way Street

Reciprocity is the way to go. When I receive validation for my ideas, I'm willing to really dig deep and discuss them and even to accept criticism. The constructive argument becomes beneficial for all because it shows communication and effective listening. We can accept people pointing out our mistakes if they also commend us for the parts that help. Bringing balance into any conversation is a hard-won reward, especially after navigating criticism and new perspectives that don't immediately line up with ours.

What have you felt when reading this book? Have you learned something that surprised you? Did you know about the stories I've shared here? Perhaps you can surprise me with your own idea of what the afterlife holds. Go ahead and let me know! Leave your reviews on the site from which you purchased *Decoding the Mystery of Life After Life*!

The Mystery Gift

This is what near-death experiences boil down to. People must acknowledge the severity of such events. NDEs are a shock to the system. When people witness the mysteries beyond death, they're practically subdued by the truth that shines around them. To come back down to Earth and be told that they witnessed a pure falsification of the mind is quite a letdown. Let's be kinder and more helpful than that!

We understand that our lives are a gift. Every day is a gift, but sometimes we need a soft push to propel us in the right direction. NDEs are neither soft nor necessarily the motivation anyone desires. But when one of us comes out the other side absolutely transformed, it's our responsibility to take that love we've experienced in the afterlife and bring it out into the world. This is the self-love and respect for our relationships that we need. If a glimpse of it can motivate someone to change the most fundamental parts of their lives, imagine what living in the truth can do for everyone.

So, let's embrace the mystery of death and the afterlife. Let's live our lives to the fullest. Who knows? Maybe one day we'll uncover the truth. But until then, revel in the uncertainty and make the most of this so-called life.

If it's a real heavenly afterlife that gives us these experiences, or if it's our brains going into overdrive to show us fantastical imagery, would you deny it? Maybe it's the cosmos where science and faith embrace and offer a gentle and even joyous transition for everyone in the end. Do I mind if it's the universe or me that shows this kindness to myself?

Share Your Thoughts

D ear Readers,

    I am writing to express my deepest gratitude for your support in reading my book. Your time and engagement mean the world to me. If you've enjoyed the journey through these pages, please consider leaving a review. Your words can guide and inspire other readers, helping them discover the book and decide if it's the right fit for them. Reviews are the lifeblood of independent authors, and your honest feedback can make a significant impact. Thank you for being a part of my literary journey, and I look forward to hearing from you.

    To submit a review, kindly navigate to your Order History, locate the book in your purchased items, and select 'Write a Product Review.' You can also use the QR code provided below if you are in the United States.

With gratitude,

Joyce T.

References

ABC News. (2012, October 25). *Neuroscientist sees "proof of heaven" in week-long coma.* https://abcnews.go.com/Health/neuroscientist-sees-proof-heaven-week-long-coma/story?id=17555207

Alexander, E. (2012). *Proof of heaven.* Simon & Schuster.

Atwater, P.M.H (1994). *Beyond the light.* Birch Lane Press.

Bacchus, G. (2021, August 19). *Resolving family grief after a bereavement.* Grief and Loss. https://www.griefandloss.co.uk/resolving-family-grief-after-a-bereavement/

Blackmore, S. (2019, October 24). *Out-of-body experiences: Mine is finally explained.* Psychology Today. https://www.psychologytoday.com/us/blog/ten-zen-questions/201910/out-body-experiences-mine-is-finally-explained

Blanke, O., Landis, T., Spinelli, L., & Seeck, M. (2004, February 1). Out-of-body experience and autoscopy of neurological origin. *Oxford Academic.* https://academic.oup.com/brain/article/127/2/243/347826?login=true

Bowman C., & Bowman S. (1995). *Interview with Dr. Ian Stevenson.* Children's Past

178

JOYCE T.

1

Lives. https://web.archive.org/web/20041001080810/h
ttp://www.childpastlives.org/stevenson_intv.htm

Carr, D., & Sharp, S. (2013, June 29). *Do afterlife beliefs affect psychological adjustment to late-life spousal loss?* National Library of Medicine. https://www.ncbi.nlm.nih.g
ov/pmc/articles/PMC3894123/

Carter, J. (2018, September 5). *New age beliefs are common in America—and in our churches.* The Gospel Coalition. https://www.thegospelcoalition.org/article/new-ag
e-beliefs-common-america-common-churches/

Chandra N. S. (2015, February 17). *Casket of stories.* Omji Publishing House.

Charlier, P. (2014, June 14). Oldest medical description of a near death experience (NDE), France, 18th century. *Resuscitation Journal.* https://www.resuscitationjournal.
com/article/S0300-9572(14)00588-7/

Colebrooke, N. (2019, October 15). *Is there life after death? This doctor thinks so.* The Click. https://theclick
.news/is-there-life-after-death-this-doctor-thinks-so/

Crawford, J. (Director). (2022). *Puss in boots: The last wish* [Film]. DreamWorks Animation.

Cretton, D.D. (Director). (2021). *Shang-Chi: The legend of the ten rings* [Film]. Marvel Studios.

Danowski, K. (n.d.). *What happens after death In Shinto?* Just About

Japan. https://justaboutjapan.com/what-happens-after-de
ath-in-shinto-understanding-the-japanese-afterlife/

Decker, J., & McAdam, E. [Cinema Therapy]. (2023, May 9). *Therapists react to Puss in boots: The last wish with guest Emma McAdam* [Video]. YouTube. https://www.youtube.com/watch?v=ssJmeqgQuVQ

Diaz, A. (2015, November 24). *"We happy you alive!": Tracy Morgan has returned.* Complex. https://www.complex.com/pop-culture/a/angel-diaz/tracy-morgan-interview-foot-locker

Durant, W. (1926). *The story of philosophy.* Simon & Schuster.

Eadie, B. (2002). *Embraced by the light.* Bantam.

Entin, E. (2021, July 12). *Following my dad's death, this research convinced me of an afterlife.* Mind Body Green. https://www.mindbodygreen.com/articles/research-on-the-afterlife

Ford, J. M. (2023, March 7). *The gift of almost drowning in Lake Kegonsa.* Psychology Today. https://www.psychologytoday.com/us/blog/close-calls-and-narrow-escapes/202302/the-gift-of-almost-drowning-in-lake-kegonsa

Georgiou, A. (2021, March 1). *Near-death experiences can "totally transform" a person in seconds says scientist.* Newsweek. https://www.newsweek.com/near-death-experiences-transform-person-seconds-scientist-1572878

Gholipour, B. (2014, July 25) *Oldest medical report of near-death experience discovered.* LiveScience. https://www.livescience.com/46993-medical-report-of-near-death-experience.html

Greyson, B. (1983, June). *The near-death experiences.* ResearchGate. https://www.researchgate.net/publication/271857657_The_Near-Death_Experience_Scale

Harrison, K. (2012). *Something deadly this way comes.* HarperCollins.

Herodotus. (1997). *Isles of the blest, elysium, white isle* (C. Parada & M. Förlag, Trans.). Maicar. (Original work published in 5th century B.C.E). https://www.maicar.com/GML/IslesBlest.html

Herrero N., Gallo, F., Gasca, M., Gleiser, P. M., & Forcato, C. (2022, April). *Spontaneous and induced out-of-body experiences during sleep paralysis.* ResearchGate. https://www.researchgate.net/publication/360223279_SPONTANEOUS_AND_INDUCED_OUT-OF-BODY_EXPERIENCES_DURING_SLEEP_PARALYSIS_EMOTIONS_AURA_RECOGNITION_AND_CLINICAL_IMPLICATIONS

Horgan, J. (2021, September 27). Death, physics and wishful thinking. *Scientific American.* https://www.scientificamerican.com/article/death-physics-and-wishful-thinking/

Johnson, K. A., Minton, E. A., & McClernon, M. P. (2023). Recycling, relatedness, and reincarnation: Religious beliefs about nature and the afterlife as predictors of sustainability practices. *Psychology of Religion and Spirituality*, 15(2), 228–240. https://doi.org/10.1037/rel0000407

Jung, C. (1934). *On life after death.* Hermetic Academy Library. https://www.hermetics.net/media-library/mysticism/carl-gustav-jung-life-death/

Kadagian, D. J., Shushan, G., & van Lomell, P. (2022). *The crossover experience.* Kindle Scribe.

Kail, T. (Director). (2020). *Hamilton* [Film]. Walt Disney Pictures; 5000 Broadway Productions; Nevis Productions; Old 320 Sycamore Pictures; RadicalMedia.

Kaleem, J. (2014, April 21). *"Heaven is for real" spurs conversations and controversy on near-death experiences.* HuffPost. https://www.huffpost.com/entry/heaven-is-for-real-near-death-experience_n_5175109

Khanna, S., & Greyson, B. (2014). *Daily spiritual experiences before and after near-death experiences.* American Psychological Association. https://www.apa.org/pubs/journals/features/rel-a0037258.pdf

Knapp, G. (2021, May 4). *I-Team: After 3 near-death experiences, local man's mission is to help dying veterans.* 8 News Now. https://www.8newsnow.com/investigators/dannionbrinkley/

Lallanilla, M. (2013, December 06). *Get naked and dig: The bizarre effects of hypothermia.* Live-

Science. https://www.livescience.com/41730-hypother
mia-terminal-burrowing-paradoxical-undressing.html

Leaviss, J., & Uttley, L. (2014, September 12). *Psy-chotherapeutic benefits of compassion-focused therapy: an early systematic review.* National Library of Medicine. https://www.ncbi.nlm.nih.gov/pmc/articles/PMC 4413786/

Long, J. (n.d.-a). *How many NDEs occur in the United States every day?* NDERF. https://www.nderf.org/NDE RF/Research/number_nde_usa.htm

Long, J. (n.d.-b). *Near death experience overview.* NDERF. https://nderf.org/NDERF/Articles/NDE%20 Overview.htm

Long, J., & Perry, P. (2010). *Evidence of the afterlife.* HarperOne.

MacIsaac, T. (2023, February 27). *How common are near-death experiences? NDEs by the numbers.* The Epoch Times. https://www.theepochtimes.com/bright/how-common-a re-near-death-experiences-ndes-by-the-numbers-757401

McKay, R. (2019, August 17). *Learn about the unique rituals of the Toraja from Indonesia.* WHO. https://www .who.com.au/what-is-toraja-death-ceremony-in-indonesia

Mehta, F. (2014, May 23). *3-year-old claims to remember who killed him in past life, leads police to body.* Wall Street Insanity. https://wallstreetinsanity.com/3-year-old-claims-to-rem ember-who-killed-him-in-past-life-leads-police-to-body/

Mika. (2022, October 22). *The Cherokee people's fascinating beliefs about death and the afterlife.* Indian Country Extension. https://www.indiancountryextension.org/the-cherok ee-peoples-fascinating-beliefs-about-death-and-the-afterlife

Miller, L. (2014, April 20). *Beyond death: The science of the afterlife.* TIME https://time.com/68381/life-beyond-d eath-the-science-of-the-afterlife-2/

Moody, R. (1975). *Life after life.* HarperOne.

Moody, R. (2015, April 25). *The founding of IANDS: Raymond Moody.* IANDS. https://www.iands.org/about/about-iands27/hist ory/the-founding-of-iands-raymond-moody.html

Moorjani, A. (2012, January 1). *Dying to be me.* Hay House, Inc.

Moshakis, A. (2021, March 7). *What do near-death experiences mean, and why do they fascinate us?* The Guardian. https://www.theguardian.com/society/2021/ma r/07/the-space-between-life-and-death

Moyra. (2022, September 22). *Quotes and poems about death, grieving, and healing.* Holidappy. https://holidappy. com/quotes/Exits-Death-Poems-and-Death-Quotes

National Geographic Society. (2023). *Jainism.* National Geographic. https://education.nationalgeographic.org/reso urce/jainism/

Plato (1997). *Isles of the blest, elysium, white isle* (C. Parada & M. Förlag, Trans.). Maicar. (Original work published in 5th century B.C.E). https://www.maicar.com/GML/IslesBlest.html

Pratchett, T. (2006). *Wintersmith.* HarperTempest.

Rice, H. S. (n.d.) *There is no night without a dawning.* Poemist. https://www.poemist.com/helen-steiner-rice/there-is-no-night-without-a-dawning

Ring, K. (1984, August 1). *Heading toward omega.* Harper Perennial.

Rodrigues, L. A. (2011, January 13). *Ex-atheist describes near-death experience.* SouthCoast Today. https://www.southcoasttoday.com/story/news/2004/01/31/ex-atheist-describes-near-death/50292715007/

Sacks, O. (2007, July 16). *A bolt from the blue.* The New Yorker. https://www.newyorker.com/magazine/2007/07/23/a-bolt-from-the-blue

Sabom, M. (1998). *Light and death: One doctor's fascinating account of near-death experiences.* Zondervan.

Schur, M., (Director) Gersten, K. (Writer), & Jefferson, C. (Writer). (2018). Somewhere else (Season 2 Episode 13) [TV series episode]. In M. Schur, D. Miner, M. Sackett, & D. Goddard (Executive Producers), *The good place.* NBC; Fremulon 3 Arts Entertainment; Universal Television.

Schweigert, M. B. (2014, July 21). *Dannion Brinkley has died three times—and lived to tell about it.* Lancaster Online.

https://lancasteronline.com/features/dannion-brinkley
-has-died-three-times-and-lived-to-tell-about-it/article_b
ad0578e-0e68-11e4-9a9f-0017a43b2370.html

Searls, D. (1994). *Yellow moon*. Samhain Publishing.

Shaw, J., Gandy, S., & Stumbrys, T. (2023). *Transformative effects of spontaneous out of body experiences in healthy individuals: An interpretative phenomenological analysis. In Psychology of Consciousness: Theory, Research, and Practice*. ResearchGate. https://www.researchgate.net/publication/369861046_Transformative_Effects_of_Spontaneous_Out_of_Body _Experiences_in_Healthy_Individuals_An_Interpretativ e_Phenomenological_Analysis

Shetty, J. [Jay Shetty Podcast]. (2023, July 10). *Tom Holland gets vulnerable about mental health & overcoming social anxiety* [Video]. YouTube. https://www.youtube.com/watch?v=GOqEl4ADyVk

Shola (Presenter). (n.d.). *What happens when we die* [Video]. BBC. https://www.bbc.co.uk/bitesize/topics/z kdk382/articles/zbgp7nb

Shunya. (2017). *Immortal talks*. Seer Books.

SSF IIIHS CONFERENCES. (2016, December 30). *MD has hellish near death experience Dr. Rajiv Parti l Lynn Fishman SSF IIIHS Conferences* [Video]. YouTube. https://www.youtube.com/watch?v=5Q8gCW_d850

Stevenson, I. (1997). *Where reincarnation and biology intersect.* Praeger Publishers. https://epdf.tips/where-rei ncarnation-and-biology-intersect.html

Storm, H. (2005). *My descent into death.* Harmony.

Sullivan, W. (2023, May 5). *Surging brain activity in dying people may be a sign of near-death experiences.* Smithsonian   Magazine. https://www.smithsonianmag.com/smart-news/surging -brain-activity-in-dying-people-may-be-a-sign-of-near-de ath-experiences-180982106/

Tamkins, T. (2023, October 7). *5 who survived cardiac arrest describe what they saw and heard before reviving.* NBC News. https://www.nbcnews.com/health/health-news/ -death-survivors-describe-saw-heard-reviving-rcna117511

Taylor, S. (2018, November 14). *Transformation through dying.* Psychology To- day. https://www.psychologytoday.com/us/blog/out-th e-darkness/201811/transformation-through-dying

Taylor, S. (2020, July 6). *David Ditchfield's remarkable near-death experience.* Psychology Today. https://www.psychologytoday.com/us/blog/out-the-dar kness/202007/david-ditchfields-remarkable-near-death-e xperience

Taylor, S. (2021, December 20). *Evaluating the evidence for reincarnation.* Psychology To-

d   a   y   .
https://www.psychologytoday.com/us/blog/out-the-dar
kness/202112/evaluating-the-evidence-reincarnation

Tedx Talks. (2013, December 1). *Dying to be me Anita Moorjani at TEDxBayArea* [Video]. YouTube. https://www.youtube.com/watch?v=rhcJNJbRJ6U

Tilles, Y. (n.d.). *Judaism and reincarnation.* Chabad. https://www.chabad.org/kabbalah/article_cdo/aid/380599/jewish/Judaism-and-Reincarnation.htm

Tucker, J. B. (2007). *Children who claim to remember previous lives: Past, present, and future research.* University of Virginia. https://med.virginia.edu/perceptual-studies/wp-content/uploads/sites/360/2015/11/REI35.pdf

van Lommel, P., van Wees, R., Meyers, V., & Elfferich, I. (2021, December 15). Near-death experience in survivors of cardiac arrest. *The Lancet, 358.* https://pimvanlommel.nl/wp-content/uploads/2017/11/Lancet-artikel-Pim-van-Lommel.pdf

Wehrstein, K. M. (2022, March 1). *Shanti Devi.* PSI Encyclopedia. https://psi-encyclopedia.spr.ac.uk/articles/shanti-devi-reincarnation-case

Wheaton, O. (2021, January 29). *Where do we go when we die? Different beliefs on the afterlife and how they affect attitudes towards death.* Marie Curie. https://www.mariecurie.org.uk/talkabout/articles/where-do-we-go-when-we-die/287832

Williams, K. (2019, September 21). *People are dramatically changed by near-death experiences*. Near-Death Experiences and the Afterlife. https://near-death.com/people-are-drama tically-changed-by-ndes/

Working With Indigenous Australians. (2020, June). *The Dreaming*. http://www.workingwithindigenousaustralians .info/content/Culture_2_The_Dreaming.html

Printed in the USA
CPSIA information can be obtained
at www.ICGtesting.com
LVHW041102031024
792827LV00016B/75

9 798869 157225